KT-447-736

How to Find It,
Build It and Change Your Life

martin amor
and alex pellew

PORTFOLIO
PENGUIN

PORTFOLIO PENGUIN

UK | USA | Canada | Ireland | Australia
India | New Zealand | South Africa

Portfolio Penguin is part of the Penguin Random House group of companies
whose addresses can be found at global.penguinrandomhouse.com.

Penguin
Random House
UK

First published 2015
002

Copyright © Martin Amor and Alex Pellew, 2015

The moral right of the authors has been asserted

Set in 9/12.75 pt ITC Stone Serif Std
Typeset by Jouve (UK), Milton Keynes
Printed in Great Britain by Clays Ltd, St Ives plc

A CIP catalogue record for this book is available from the British Library

ISBN: 978–0–241–01483–7

To Anita, my amazing wife-to-be, the cornerstone of our family and the making of me. Thank you for your patience, understanding and support as I snatched moments around family life to write this book. And to Sofia, my beautiful, strong-minded and funny daughter. I can't wait to see the amazing idea you have inside you.

A.P.

To Jaime, who taught me to shoot for the stars.

M.A.

Alas for those that never sing,
But die with all their music in them.

Oliver Wendell Holmes

contents

preface

These days we are all creators.

Powerful computers sit on our laps connecting us to millions of other people in seconds. Affordable software makes it easier than ever to design websites, edit movies, create compelling images, write books and sell what we make to a global audience.

Yet for most of us, our ideas stay in our heads mingling with thoughts of dinner and telly, stuck behind mental barriers of our own making:

'Only people who are more creative than me make their ideas happen.'

'I'm not a born entrepreneur like the ones on TV – how will I know what to do?'

'I'm just not the sort to take a leap of faith like that. I'd better stick to what I know.'

But if you choose to start, and arm yourself with just a handful of simple tools, steps and behaviours, and put one foot in front of the other, you can – you will – change your life with your idea.

Whatever your idea ends up being – a new gadget, a hit TV show, a craft event in your village hall or the next Facebook – the process of bringing it into being will change your life.

Your idea will inspire a sense of purpose in you. It will show you what you can do, displaying the world and your place in it through a new lens. It will sharpen your sense of your own power and – in time, with persistence – it will offer you the freedom to live the life you want.

All you need to do is start . . .

introduction

A story you might recognize

It's Tuesday morning.

You are sitting at your desk, knee-deep in emails.

You smile and take a minute to reflect fondly on your moment of genius last night . . .

As you struggled in through the front door laden with shopping, it came to you.

'Bin bags!'

You had done almost everything right. You had scribbled a note on your little blackboard when you realized you were running out. You had even made a mental note as you left work heading for the supermarket that evening. But, crucially, the words 'bin' and 'bags' had not been added to a shopping list.

So, for another few days at least, the kitchen would be graced with that bulging Sainsbury's bag hanging off the door under the sink.

You allowed yourself a few seconds of self-loathing – but then something shifted.

Wait.

What if I could programme my phone to ping up a reminder when I'm at the supermarket – when I am at the place where I actually need to remember the damn things? What if, as I cross the threshold, a message pings up on my screen: 'BIN BAGS!'

This is gold!

Why has no one thought of this before?

Even without a shopping list, that roll of tie-handle fifty-litre bags would find its way into my trolley.

Damn it, this is dynamite!

Everyone needs one of these – A LOCATION-BASED REMINDER!

You've found a perfectly elegant solution to one of modern life's most enduring problems: forgetting things when you go to the supermarket. Your mind plays the movie of a future when you're the toast of the tech world and millions of forgetful people follow your hilarious wisdom on Twitter, when your company is awash with cash thanks to the thousands of daily downloads of your life-changing app.

You luxuriate in the possibilities around your location-based reminder:

- What could it be called?
- What will it look like?
- How much should I sell it for?

This is exhilarating. The Location-Based Reminder idea will surely change your life. You've always known you have special creativity and energy. Finally, you are realizing your potential. You head to Godaddy to check for available domain names.

A few days later, the movie in your mind has changed. Where there were once images of yachts and ski lodges, there is now only a list of difficult questions:

- Err, how do you make an app?
- What if someone else has thought of it? Surely Google is on to this.
- How many people would actually buy it anyway?
- Can I afford to leave my job?
- Will I have enough money to make it work?
- Do I really want to spend the next couple of years making an app?
- What will people say when I tell them that I – probably the most forgetful person they know – want to develop a reminder?

A couple of conversations with friends reinforce your doubts and, before you can whisper 'maybe this time it will be different', this idea has joined the others you won't get round to taking any further. Instead of changing your life, the location-based reminder has become further evidence that you're not the type to make your idea happen. Anyway, you reassure yourself, life isn't all bad. You've got a roof over your head and an OK job. Why put a big challenge like this into the mix – especially when it looks like it might not work?

Now – back to those emails.

We did it, so can you

We've been having ideas too – for years. In fact, our ideas have made millions. For other people.

We have spent much of our careers helping big companies become richer, including Nike, Telefonica, Unilever, Mars, Pepsico, Fosters, Prudential, SK Telecom (Korea), Samsung, Nestlé, Heineken, Carlsberg, Virgin, Pernod Ricard, Shell and InterContinental Hotel Group.

We work on their tough questions:

- What will our new breakthrough product be?
- How are we going to top last year's performance?
- How will we fight off the threat of our competitors' new technology?
- How can we expand our audience to include younger people?
- How can we turn this new technology into a product lots of people will buy?

We have always had to work fast, so we have learned techniques that solve problems like these and quickly every time.

In the last few years, we have started to wonder how what we have learned could help people as well as companies. We can help an organization develop a new product that sells millions, so surely we can help a person find an idea and turn it into something that will change their life.

We decided to test our techniques on ourselves – and committed to realizing our own ideas first. These are now growing businesses having a positive impact on the world, and we both have high hopes for the future. You can find out more about our ideas at theideainyou.com if you're interested.

We now believe that these techniques have the potential to make a huge and positive change in many people's lives. We're confident that they will help you negotiate your freedom and make your dreams come true. To us this will mean at least as much as developing a new packaged coffee for a blue-chip multinational, a clever flu remedy concept for a pharmaceutical company or a new credit card idea for a bank.

We had never seen ourselves as entrepreneurs. We had always assumed that we would work for other people, and for many years we did. Now we know that we can turn ideas we care about into businesses, and that we can thoroughly enjoy it. We know because we've tried, finally. And, because we've come to this a little late, we have developed missionary zeal about it.

We've had such a positive experience developing our ideas that we want to help you find yours. We want to help you find something you care about and take the first steps in creating something amazing out of it.

Since getting started on our own businesses, we have become curious about what it takes for anyone to do it. So we have gone out and spoken to a range of people leading their own small but growing concerns in the worlds of breakfast, interior design, teaching coding, mass-participation events, pizza, finance, halal ready-meals, bicycles, rainwear, juice, coffee and chocolate, among others. How did they come up with their ideas in the first place? How were they turning their daydreams into reality? What obstacles had they encountered? What techniques did they find most useful? What do they wish they'd known back when they started?

We spoke to introverts and extroverts, to people with years of previous experience and to some who had none. Some had money to spend; some had hardly any. Some were long on confidence;

some more reticent about their abilities. All, though, were delighted by what they were achieving and – happily for us – keen to share what they had learned.

We decided we needed a term to describe them other than 'entrepreneurs'. We wanted a name that was more positive, that would imply making something that would change the world, something we would be happy to call ourselves. For the purposes of this book and the community around this book, we are going to use the word **creators**.

Even though you may not see yourself as an entrepreneur, you are a creator. The urge you are feeling now to move things forward is one sign of this. Your choosing to read this book is another. There is an idea in you waiting to come out. You may not know how to do it yet, or even what it will be, but you know it will change things – for you and for the world.

You only have to look around you to see that human beings are by nature creators: houses, sofas, computers, paintings, wallpapers, carpets, TV shows, magazines, websites, jams, pickles, pastas, knives, forks, clothes – all these started life as someone's idea. Whoever came up with the design, script or concept behind any one of them was a creator. They had an idea, they cared enough about it to get started, they overcame whatever barriers existed and put one foot in front of the other until their idea became real.

You might think this is not likely to happen to you. You might have decided that you are too lazy / too low in confidence / too short of cash / too tired / too old / too young / too frightened of failure / too stuck in your ways / too undereducated / too overeducated / too awkward around other people / too bad at being on your own / too useless at communicating / too *whatever* to be a creator.

You might believe that because you prefer sitting on the sofa eating HobNobs to doing things you will never bring your idea to fruition, or that you don't know enough about anything, let alone about how to build something. You might have decided that you just aren't the type to make a success of anything, since you have never yet done so. Or perhaps you haven't had an idea to speak of for years, so how on earth could you find one you care about now? Perhaps in your mind this is something only other people do, and people like you should shuffle back to the sofa and pick up those HobNobs and stick the telly on, because you could never bring an idea to life.

If this is you, or even partly you, read on. We have written this book for you. Actually, we've written it for who we were a few years ago. We were on that proverbial sofa surrounded by biscuit crumbs – letting other people take the benefit of the work we did every day, believing that building something original and success-ful was something only other people did.

These days we still doubt our abilities and we still find ourselves drawn to the sofa – but we can also report that, if you're anything like us, you can do this. With an idea you care about, some simple steps to follow and a little awareness, you can resist the tendency to be a procrastinating biscuit-eating layabout. You can – and you *will* – develop something significant of your own. In our case, we've even managed to convince a reputable publisher that we can write a book about it. So – it turns out you don't need to be like those shouty apprentices on the telly. You can be you and still do it. We are all creators.

We should say that very few ideas will bring forth the fame or wealth of Steve Jobs or Mark Zuckerberg. There are – so far – no yachts or ski lodges on our insurance schedules or on those of the creators we have spoken to, but we are all agreed that creating something new that people find useful is extremely gratifying and utterly life-changing.

Imagine:

- You've learned to believe that you can do this.
- You've found an idea you are excited about. It feels right for you to pursue. You believe it's important to do it.
- You've started modestly but you're seeing positive change. You're thrilled that your idea is out in the world.
- You're risking very little. You're keeping your costs low by using

free resources where possible. You're careful to fit your idea into your life, making sure that you don't put the things you value at risk.

- Quietly, you have a dream of how things will look when your idea blows up. You know it won't do that overnight. You know you will have to put in energy over time – but you allow yourself this adventure in your mind, because it keeps you going. It pulls you towards a future you are excited about.
- You've played around with different ways of talking about your idea, and you're getting a good feel for what people love about it and why.
- You can see that your idea is generating some *social* energy – people are interested in it. They're 'liking' it, 'sharing' it and talking about it.
- Little by little, you are improving your idea, and as you do this your confidence in yourself and your project is growing. You are learning more about how the world works.
- From time to time, of course, things don't go as planned, but you regroup, and you keep going, grateful for the experience and stronger in your desire to carry on.
- You're putting a lot of energy in, and you're getting a lot back too. People are giving you feedback and you're starting to get good news – sales, positive reviews, and PR.
- You see inspiration everywhere you look: ideas, resources and technologies which change how you think about your idea and what you want to do to make it grow.
- You have a good feeling about it. You know that your idea will indeed change the world. It is already doing so in its own small way – and it's been changing you since day one.

Our goal is for this to be your story.

But before you quit your job, or make the down-payment on your shop, or spend money on a fancy logo or website for your new product or book or business or shop or event or service – tempting though it is – please take a little time to read this book.

With the techniques in this book, and the awareness that you will develop as you try them, and with a little application (actually a lot of application, but don't worry: we'll help you with that too), you will turn your daydream into dynamite. It will take time, and it will ask a lot of you, but it will be one of the most inspiring and energizing experiences of your life.

Still doubting?

In case you still doubt your ability to do this, here are our responses to the worries people usually have when we talk to them about getting started:

I don't have an idea. That's OK. We'll show you how to find one that you care about deeply and can't wait to get into.

I'm not creative – I can't come up with good ideas. With the right processes and a bit of awareness about where ideas come from, everyone is creative. We are not painting Picassos here. We are finding something you want to do, and taking the first joyous steps in doing it. You can do this – everyone can.

But I don't know much about business. You don't need to. You can learn that later. At this stage we are interested in character more than knowledge. This process takes passion, energy and awareness more than experience. Stay true to your own values – and use the techniques in this book to work towards your dreams. In time, your idea will teach you everything you need to know about business and much else besides.

I have an idea but I'm not sure people will like it. That's normal. We will show you how to get your idea out of your head and into the world, so you can start learning about it. This process will sharpen your thinking about your idea fast. You will soon develop confidence in it – or make room for a better one. We'll also show you how to overcome the fear of failure that we all feel as we put our ideas out into the world.

I don't know if I really want to do this. It is wise to be thinking like that. You will really need to want it or it won't happen. We will share how to find an idea you care about, how to understand the change you want to see in the world, and how to explore how your idea will help you do that. Then you'll want to do it.

I'm worried someone else has got there first. This is one of the most common fears we hear. Our answer is always the same. All you can do is focus your energy on finding an idea that is right for you and doing your best to make it shine. Everything else will fall into place.

I don't have enough money to get my idea going. That is actually good news. With limited resources, you will have to start small and learn steadily. You will have to take your time exploring what is at the heart of your idea, and what is surplus to requirements. You will build something you understand and that works well without wasting money.

You may need more resources and help from other people in time. If you've grown steadily, you'll know your stuff – and will understand exactly what you need and why, and how to ask for it.

Is now a good time for me to do this? For the individual, there has never been a better time to make an idea happen.

Today you can do all the following for free:

- Post videos online to a potential audience of 2.25 billion.
- Create a shop which people all over the world can buy from.
- Tell the world what you are thinking right now.
- Show the world what your product looks like, even without a website of your own.

As these tools are being picked up by a community of creators around the world, so there are more and more people to collaborate with, more exciting things happening from these encounters, better tools to support them happening, and stronger role models appearing. Now is the perfect time for the millions of individuals who want to set themselves free with an idea.

In our line of work, we've noticed that companies are spending fortunes just to learn how to move faster than they do now. They want to be more experimental in their approach, closer to the end user and living their ideas rather than just executing them. These big powerful companies with massive overheads and complex reporting structures want to be more like us! It's our time. Let's take advantage!

Will this book really change my life? We've designed this book to be as practical and as inspiring as possible. It's a series of steps – from getting your head straight and finding an idea you care about to getting crystal clear about what it is and putting it out into the world so you can make waves with it. We explain what to expect, how to think and what to do – one step at a time.

There are effectively two journeys that you'll go through simultaneously. One is your own, as you clarify what you want to do and build your belief that you can do it. The other is your idea's, as you develop it, share it with the world and improve it over time, attracting fans, generating sales and developing the model for its success.

These changes won't occur if all you do is read a book. Your understanding and your beliefs will change a little, but your idea will still be floating around in your head, or stuck on the fridge on a piece of paper. If you want the wonderful benefits of creating something – you must *do*. In fact, you must become *excellent* at doing. So let's get into how to do that now.

DO IT NOW

A boy stands on a high diving board.

He shuffles towards the edge, looking out. The sound of other swimmers fades away. He takes a deep breath and looks down at the parallel lines on the bottom of the pool, the blue of the water and the ripples on its surface.

He stands, frozen.

The psychological term for what the boy is experiencing is 'preparedness'. It's a survival mechanism. Should I or shouldn't I? It has been a helpful buffer between seeing the options and deciding to act for a couple of million years. We take a look at our options and make a call about what to do. If we're good at spotting the risks, we're more likely to survive. If we're too good, we'll never do anything.

The boy on the diving board is weighing up two very different paths. Option 1 and he leaps off the diving board, soars through the air and splashes down safely. Option 2 and he decides to head down the ladder, with a sense of disappointment and perhaps returns later for a second try.

Whenever we weigh up our options for action, we get a few moments when our lives could go one way or the other. This happens even when we're weighing up whether to pick up the phone and make a call, or when we're considering whether we should turn the TV off. Those few milliseconds as we choose what to do next are critical. Jump or don't jump. Turn the TV off and get on with a project we are working on, or just stay sitting on the sofa doing very little. These are turning points.

There is a way of managing these critical moments, and it's an essential behaviour for you to adopt if you want to enjoy the benefits of making anything happen. We call it '**DO IT NOW**', and it works like this:

Whenever you are thinking about something you want to do, **DO IT NOW**. Not later on this evening or tomorrow or at the weekend. Now. Switch from weighing up your options into action deliberately and immediately.

Instead of hunting around for reasons not to do something, you just do it. In the case of the boy on the diving board, it's the equivalent of him climbing the ladder, walking to the edge and jumping straight off. No hanging around and getting stuck in 'shall I, shan't I?' mode. Just get on with it. Now.

Pretty straightforward, isn't it?

What we've noticed in our years of practising **DO IT NOW** is that the more you do it – even on things you've done a thousand times before, like doing the washing-up, filling up the ice-cube trays or putting out the bins – the better you get at it.

If you don't **DO IT NOW**, you add what you need to do to your to-do list. You carry one more task around with you for the rest of the day: one more thing to do, sapping your energy. If you jump and **DO IT NOW**, it's amazing how much easier the thing you need to do becomes. It just happens.

This is the case especially if you're worried about a task: **DO IT NOW**! It will immediately be less of a concern, because you've started. You'll wonder what you were worrying about. Spend five minutes on it and move things on. The world will look different and you'll be clearer on what you need to do next.

For the creator – for you – the ability to act is central to this amazing, unpredictable journey. Without the simple act of doing (even if it's for only five minutes) you're not making the idea in you happen; you're just reading a book and thinking about what it would be like if you did. While we hope that this is a good book to read, we are much more hopeful that you will change the world. If you want to change anything, you will have to do – again and again and again, and when you don't really feel like it as well as when you do.

You can practise '**DO IT NOW**' with anything. Next time you find yourself thinking 'I really must give Bob a call', you have the opportunity to practise it. In those few seconds, as that thought passes through your mind, in that moment of mental triage, you have options. You can defer the task, making a mental note to remember that you need to make the call and go through the whole damn thing again later, or you can pick up the phone now and call Bob. Done.

The energy it will take to call now is less than the burden you'll feel each time you remember that you really ought to make that call. And what's more, once you've done it you will have moved the world on. You'll have found out Bob's news, you'll have reminded yourself how much you enjoy talking to him, you might even have got some suggestions from him about how you could make your idea better.

Doing is always something that has to take place now. You making a success of your idea, your ability to learn, the possibility of creating any outcomes at all – *all* of these depend on your willingness to do. Now. With each little bit of action, you bring yourself a little closer to achieving what you need to do.

Doing beats talking every time

I thought about it in my head and I felt it in my heart and I longed for it to happen with all of my soul – but I made it with my hands.

Rob Ryan, visual artist

Thinking and talking are always fleeting. They may change minds but they will only change the world if they are followed by action.

In the worlds we've worked in for much of our professional lives, there has been a tendency to overvalue 'the thinking'. In these cultures, 'doing the thinking' is seen by some as more impressive than doing the doing. There are few more depressing sights than a room full of people trying to appear smarter than each other, where no one's really up for doing anything. In our years of working with big companies, we've seen it many times.

This isn't going to be the case for you and your idea. Making your own idea is the perfect arena for doing, across a wide range of activities. At most workplaces, there are many departments, but where you're going to work, there's just you. As CEO, commander-in-chief, president or whatever you want to be called in your new world, you are going to do the talking, the thinking *and* the doing.

So, since you are not (yet) a multinational corporation, and because no one is paying you to look clever, and because you want to actually move the game on rather than be a Head of Strategy, here is a suggestion:

Think, and talk, by all means to work out what you are going to do. But then – once you've finished talking – start doing!

Maybe you've always thought of yourself as someone who

doesn't get things done, or you've convinced yourself that you are lazy or frightened of committing to tasks; if so, don't worry – remember, this is a skill you can practise. It gets easier every time you do it. You just have to DO IT NOW.*

We have called the activities we ask you to do in each chapter DO IT NOW for this reason. If you do them immediately, you will move the game on. Instead of sloping off down the diving-board ladder, you'll jump screaming through the air – and it will change your life.

The word 'now' is like a bomb through the window, and it ticks.

Arthur Miller, *After the Fall*

· DO IT NOW ·

Practise DO IT NOW now! Think of something you've been meaning to get round to. You might have been putting off writing to a friend you haven't seen for a while, or you might need to tidy the kitchen or make an appointment for the dentist. Whatever you know you ought to do, put down this book and do it. Now.

---

* 'DO IT NOW' does, however, come with one caveat. It is still wise to prepare for significant tasks – for important conversations or performances, for instance. It's always good to think about how to do something well. But use this as a means to make what you do excellent rather than a reason for inaction. If you know how to do a task and the only thing stopping you is inertia . . . DO IT NOW! If you don't know how to do something, start working out how to do it – but, again, DO IT NOW!

Laying the Groundwork

GETTING YOUR HEAD STRAIGHT

The world as we have created it is a process of our thinking. It cannot be changed without changing our thinking. Albert Einstein

It's 31 March 1973 in the San Diego Sports Arena. A crowd of almost twelve thousand is watching as Muhammad Ali steps into the ring. He's wearing a white rhinestone-encrusted robe with 'People's Choice' appliquéd on the back, a gift from Elvis Presley.

Ali is 5-1 on favourite.

His opponent is staring at the canvas.

Ali's challenger is a virtual unknown called Ken Norton. He weighed in at 210lb this afternoon, some 11lb lighter than Ali, and this evening is set to earn six times more than he has ever earned from a fight – still less than a quarter of Ali's guaranteed $210,000.

Ken Norton would be forgiven for thinking he doesn't stand a chance. In fact, he is thinking quite the opposite. This evening, as he stands in the ring preparing for the biggest bout of his life, Norton has these words in his mind:

Life's battles don't always go to the stronger or faster man, but sooner or later the man who wins is the man who thinks he can.

Years later, Norton explained that his thoughts that night were from one of the earliest self-help books, *Think and Grow Rich* by

Napoleon Hill. Published in 1937, it shares the mindset of the successful industrialist. For twenty years, Hill, the author, had interviewed the most eminent businessmen of the time. He wanted to work out how they did it.

The men he got to know (for they were all men) were spectacularly successful: Henry Ford, William Wrigley Jr, Charles M. Schwab, John D. Rockefeller and Thomas Edison among others. Trillionaires in today's money. What he discovered about them was this: it was not their means, skills or experience that set them apart; it was how they thought.

Hill put it like this: 'Thoughts are things, and powerful things at that, when they are mixed with definiteness of purpose, persistence and a BURNING DESIRE [his capitals] for their translation into riches, or other material things.'

In other words, if you can create exactly what you want in your mind, and make it huge, you can move towards it. Whatever you want, if you can think it, you can have it.

Ken Norton broke Muhammad Ali's jaw in the eleventh round. He was crowned North American Boxing Federation Heavyweight Champion. Ali never wore the sparkly robe again.

Like Ken Norton, you may be an outsider. You may have limited means, skills or experience in the game of finding an idea and making it grow. You may see more in front of you that is unknown than known. You could reasonably choose to believe that you are not going to succeed. Or – like Ken Norton – you can decide to focus on what you want, and make yourself believe in it so deeply that it burns white hot in your mind – and then persist until it becomes reality.

You have sixty thousand thoughts a day. What are yours telling you? Ignore for a moment the operational ones like 'shoes after socks' and 'brush your teeth before bed'. What are the important ones telling you – the ones about you and your future?

Yours might fill you with confidence about the future. They might inspire you to make great things happen in your life. They might tell you that you are the perfect person to make an idea happen, and that you are going to change the world beyond recognition.

If this is you, you can skip this chapter.

If your thoughts generally tell you that you're really not the type to do this, that you might just read this book (or perhaps just the first couple of chapters) and then carry on with life as before – then read on.

'So I train for my fights,' Norton said, 'mentally as well as physically. One thing I do is only watch films of the fights in which I've done well or in which my opponent has done poorly.'

Ken Norton always got his head straight before a bout. He would systematically feed his mind positive thoughts, and eject negative ones the second they appeared. Unlike many other boxers, he didn't try to stare down his opponent during pre-fight announcements. Instead, he looked at the canvas and thought relentlessly and positively about winning.

We think before we do. Before every decision and every conversation, our thoughts are there – shaping what happens next. If you have your thinking working for you, good things will occur. If you can do what Ken Norton did, and feed your mind a consistently powerful positive message, you will give your idea the highest-grade rocket fuel for blasting it into orbit.

Your mind is your most important tool as you work on your idea – more important than any computer, shop or screwdriver. If it is creating positive thoughts and resisting negative ones, you will be able to create something incredible. It might surprise you that this is within your control – and in this chapter we are going to explain how you can do it.

Directing your movie

You are sitting in a cinema, in the front row. Up on the screen in front of you, a movie is playing – a colliding series of clips creating a hectic collage on the screen.

The images are bright and changing every few seconds. The sound fills the auditorium. As you watch, you become aware you are watching a movie of your life – edited moments of the past and future.

Among the scenes are moments of joy and peace. You enjoy watching them, feeling your breath lengthen and your shoulders relax.

Other moments are less comfortable for you. Scenes of shame, fear and distress. You feel a heaviness in your chest.

You become aware that every scene in this movie is shaping you – creating your hopes, fears and tendencies.

Some of the scenes are all too familiar. You've known for some time the impact they have had on how you think and feel these days. Others are more surprising: you hadn't even realized the power that they have over you – but you notice it now.

Now you zoom out, and position yourself twenty rows back. The 'you' in the front row is still there. You can see their head silhouetted and the light on their shoulders.

From here, twenty rows back, you are watching yourself watching the movie you run in your head about yourself.

What do you think that person is experiencing down there? What episodes from their life in the past are strong in their movie about themselves? What are they imagining about their future? What are they feeling when they see these scenes? Which scenes in their movie are strongest in shaping the way they see the world and how they view their place in it?

Now you zoom out again. This time you find yourself up in the projector suite, sitting behind the glass. It's quieter up here. You can see the cone of light projecting from the lens, passing through the glass and out into the cinema. You can still see yourself down there in the front row, watching the movie.

You watch yourself again for a while longer.

You're starting to get a bit of distance now. You're realizing what it must be like for that person down there. You're wondering which scenes are helping and which ones aren't.

Now zoom out again – this time you float up into the sky above the cinema, then higher still above the city and finally above the whole country, as you look down on thousands of cinemas, each with a person sitting in the front row, their faces lit up by the movie they are running of their lives.

Finally, you return to the projection booth.

You reach over to the projector and press 'PAUSE'.

What are you running in your movie? What images are you

creating about your life so far and the future you expect for yourself? How helpful are these images, memories and predictions? Are they giving you Ken Norton-like reserves of strength and resolve or are they filling you with doubt and fear about the path ahead?

The good news is that you can control them. You can notice them as they come up so they don't hijack you, you can resist the poisonous ones and you can replace them with thoughts that fill you with confidence and belief. You can alter the story you are feeding your brain.

In a moment we will look at how your mental picture of yourself is built and we'll share a range of techniques you can use to change it, but first we want to look at the role of your body.

Your body is sending messages to your brain constantly. Your brain receives the messages, interprets them and makes decisions about what to do – often without your conscious mind getting involved.

- I'm cold.
- Ouch, that hurts!
- That feels good.
- I'm hungry.

A physical signal leads to a mental response. Your body is like a radar detector for the brain, noticing what is happening and sending signals the brain can respond to. If you can control the signal your body sends, you can decide the response you want your brain to have. You can use your body to tell your brain how you are feeling.

Try this:

Notice your posture. How are you sitting or standing?

Now try this:

Round your shoulders and lower your gaze. Turn the sides of your mouth down.

Frown.

Turn your feet in towards each other.

Cross your arms.

How do you feel now? Try really hard to feel confident while you're in that position. Stay in that position – and think of yourself scoring a deciding penalty in a World Cup Final.

Not easy, huh?

Now shake out your body a little and get ready to try a new posture.

Stand or sit up straight. Push your shoulders back. Lift your chin a little. Focus on the distance. Look proud. Pull your belly button in towards your spine.

Notice how you feel in your body.

Now – what is the change in your thoughts? What are you thinking now?

Breathe it in. Enjoy the feeling.

Now open your arms above your head and look up to the heavens.

Feels good, right?

Your body is sending a signal to your brain that you are fearless, that you are brimming with hope and belief.

For some extra amusement, stay as you are with your proud posture, and try to feel weak. Try to feel completely pathetic. Not easy! Whatever signal your body gives, the mind responds accordingly. While you are in this position it's going to be very hard to feel low on confidence.

OK, now you've got your body helping, let's have a look at the brain's role in getting your head straight.

What's on your brain map?

We are showered with data every day for the whole of our lives. It's like a lifelong meteor storm of events and information. It's so intense, in fact, that the brain simply can't cope with it. It can't possibly take in every single event, conversation and thought we've experienced since birth so instead it works on a summary.

Over the years you have subconsciously cherry-picked what you considered important and stored it to create a representation of the world. Let's call this your 'brain map'. We've all got one. It's your mental representation of how the world works, and your place in it. It's your take on the world, if you like.

Our brain maps are shaped by our lives. Key moments and conversations over the years colour our assumptions and beliefs about who we are and how the world works. Events when we were young, in particular, tend to have the most impact on our maps. Any experience that packs an emotional charge will change it, for better or for worse.

Let's look at an example. Say you were unlucky enough to be bitten by a dog when you were small. It was a freak incident, but it was a seriously significant experience for you as a relatively young person. Because there was so much energy in that moment for you, your brain sensibly drew some conclusions from it. Now when you're walking to the bus stop and you see a dog – even years later – alarm bells ring inside your head. It's your brain map telling you something – reminding you that 'Dogs are dangerous!' Your brain is trying to keep you alive. Sensibly, you cross the road.

Your friend has a different map. He has only had positive experiences with dogs, so his brain map says dogs are friendly and fun. While you're crossing the road, he's stopping to say hello to the dog. This looks like madness to you, of course. Your map wants to protect you from being bitten by the dog. His doesn't have the same picture of the world as yours – he has experienced nothing that would put that message on there.

So, what is your brain map telling you? How has your mind made sense of the world and your place in it? In particular, what do you think it is routinely telling you about your ability to make your idea happen?

Perhaps it includes this story:

You are not like those clever entrepreneurs on the TV so you're going to struggle. To make something happen yourself, you will need far more experience, and probably more money and guts.

Perhaps your map has a tendency to be simplistic and unfair to you:

You'll never make anything of yourself because you're not smart enough and you don't stick with things.

You're the forgetful one in this family – only the others are going to do something great with their lives.

People always laugh at you when you make mistakes so you'd better not try anything challenging.

Or perhaps it is drawing on your past to paint a sorry picture of how things will turn out:

You haven't ever really succeeded at anything, so you probably never will.

You don't have to be Einstein to realize that if your brain map looks like that, and you don't challenge it or work hard to ignore it, you are more likely to stay on the sofa than change the world.

Even just noticing what your map says causes it to start losing its power over you. You become free to see things as they really are. You learn to notice what your map is trying to say, and to decide whether it's worth listening to. You can learn to override its constraints.

Each time you resist your map's advice, you become less likely to be hijacked by it in future. In time, you start to do things you never thought possible, even though your brain long ago decided you couldn't. You stop cowering and you approach that dog. You let it smell your hand, and give it a stroke, even though your brain map is screaming at you not to.

Understanding what your brain map is trying to tell you and then deciding whether you want to listen to it is the psychological work behind realizing your idea. Your brain map might want to derail you, and you need to be alert to this. You need to be able to spot any unhelpful stuff it is trying to tell you, and understand that it is not reality. It is just your map – your summary of the world. The first step in being able to do this is to understand how your brain map was drawn.

How are our brain maps drawn?

While you are bombarded by the data overload that is day-to-day life, there are three things your brain does as it draws its map.

1. The brain *deletes* things as they arrive
As we've discussed, our brains can't process everything they receive. One of the things the brain does to manage the heavy influx of information is to make decisions about what is important and to ignore the bits it thinks are irrelevant.

Here's what that looks like:

Martin: *I'll never make my idea happen. I'm too lazy.*
Alex: *But you've written a book – how can that be lazy?*
Martin: *Yes, but that doesn't count. It took ages, and I was checking the internet the whole time. I didn't do it on my own, either.*

And so, Martin's brain cunningly discounts some compelling evidence that he's not lazy. For whatever reason, Martin's map wants to tell him he's lazy, and he's sticking to it.

What else might he be ignoring because it doesn't fit with his map? And – importantly – what might have changed if he had interpreted his writing the book as a sign of his persistence and industry instead of ignoring it completely?

2. The brain *distorts* events
In their efforts to make sense of the world, our brains routinely change the meaning of received information, like this:

Martin: *Alex, you're one of the most industrious people I've ever met.*
Alex: *Wow, thanks!* [Thinking] *Martin obviously thinks I'm boring . . .*

And so Alex's brain transforms a well-intentioned compliment about Alex's incredible ability to move the game on into something that is effectively an insult. Martin was saying something nice, but Alex's brain has distorted Martin's compliment, probably so that it will fit with his view of himself.

3. The brain *generalizes*

Our brains tend to interpret one-off high-energy events as evidence of a much broader pattern – just like that five-year-old bitten by a dog whose brain map tells him to avoid all dogs for ever following that one unfortunate moment. When you hear yourself saying 'never' or 'always', you're probably giving yourself a dose of generalization:

Martin: *The wheels* always *fall off when I try to do new things. When I was twelve, I wanted to organize a shop at school but I forgot to bring the change box with me, so I couldn't sell anything. Everyone laughed at me. Seriously – keep me away from organizing things. I've* never *been good at it.*

Martin has expanded a single event into something much broader, carelessly reinterpreting it as a general pattern. You've NEVER been good at it, Martin? *Never*? The wheels ALWAYS fall off? Really? Imagine what Martin could achieve if he could see that day in the playground for what it was: just a one-off mistake that he can learn from rather than a reason to avoid organizing anything.

This is how our brains create the maps in our heads. We delete things that we don't want to hear, we distort things so that they fit with our picture of the world, and we generalize so we don't have to think too much.

Our maps hold a freakishly strong sway over our thinking and hence what we choose to do. There are at least five ways we can reduce their power over us, all of which transform our thinking and therefore our ability to do things:

1. We can notice our thoughts as they come up

Psychologists call this 'meta-cognition' – noticing where your thoughts tend to go. If you can notice your thoughts, you can send the unhelpful ones packing and you can use the supportive ones to inspire you. This is your secret weapon on this journey – harnessing your thoughts to help you.

Try this now.

Notice yourself as you are now, reading this book. Feel the subtle pressures on your body: the effects of gravity, your clothes on your skin, the pressure of the seat or bed beneath you.

Now scan your body up and down, focusing on the sensations you are feeling for a few moments. Try to see past the gross sensations to the subtle buzzing on your skin.

Now move your attention to your breathing. As you inhale think 'One' and as you exhale think 'Two'. One. Two. Put the book down and keep this up for a minute or so, just noticing your breathing – One (inhale) Two (exhale). Go on – **DO IT NOW**!

OK – meta-moment over. What happened? Unless you're a Zen master (and even if you are), you probably found that your thoughts drifted off somewhere.

What were those thoughts? You might have been thinking, 'This is crazy New Age nonsense – I want my money back!' or, 'I do this every day, I love meditating,' or you might have been thinking about some operational details in your life, such as what you need to get from the supermarket. Whatever your thoughts were, try to remember them.

What was the nature of those thoughts? Were they supportive? Were they neutral? Or were they unhelpful to you? How did they leave you feeling?

It's amazing how much activity there can be going on in the mind, even without our being aware of it. These are all clues about what is on your map. When you sit on the bus, or have a shower, and you realize your mind has been on a bit of an adventure, try reversing back through the thoughts you had. Make a mental note of where they went and how helpful they were to you.

With practice, your ability to 'go meta' like this will grow. You will become more aware of your thoughts as they come up in the moment. You will be able to perform a sort of triage on them, a bit like a staff nurse deciding who needs treatment, who can wait and who needs to be ejected. Was that thought helpful? If it was, it's welcome. If it wasn't, show it the door.

And once you get quite practised at it, meta-cognition becomes a parallel process – something that you have running alongside whatever you're doing in your life. You're living your life, but you're noticing your thoughts as they come up in parallel. Here's an example:

> You walk into the office one morning and your colleague says to you, 'Jeez, you look tired!' You feel a slight flash of anger come up, perhaps a bit of heat in your chest and up the back of your neck. You're half-tempted to tell him he looks as ugly as he did yesterday and you'll get a good night's sleep tonight. But, you notice this thought. You take a moment, realizing that's not going to help if you do that. Well done, you – you've gone meta: you've noticed your thinking and caught it just in time, just before you do something you might regret. You resist the urge to hit your colleague with your clever comeback. You mentally pat yourself on the back, smile at your colleague, say, 'Really? Well, *you* look great!' and head to the coffee machine, resolving to get a bit more sleep tonight.

This ability to notice your thoughts is central to your ability to deal with the challenges you will face as you proceed. Because if you control your thoughts, you can control your actions.

2. We can thank our unhelpful thoughts for their loving support and then ignore them
On the whole, our brain maps are trying to keep us safe. They include a catalogue of all the things that have affected us in the past and our thoughts draw on them, so that we don't make the same mistakes again.

Even thoughts as negative as 'You'll never do anything significant with your life' have positive intent. Believe it or not, even though they hold us back, they are actually trying to help. They are like an inner grandparent, smothering us with their love because they fear we will hurt ourselves. They don't mean to stop us making our dreams come true; they just want us to stay where they can see us, sitting safely at home in front of the TV with a jam sandwich and a nice cup of tea – because we can't hurt ourselves there. They want us to stay safe.

Whatever their intent, though, such protection has stopped being useful. Now you are intent on creating something original and significant, you don't need to stay where you are; you need to move forward. You need to try new things, which means putting yourself in harm's way as far as Grandma Don't-Ever-Change sees it. You need to put down your jam sandwich and your cup of tea, and go outside and start doing stuff you haven't done before. You need to put yourself at risk as far as she's concerned. If you don't – you will never get your idea off the ground.

Those old thoughts had better get out of the way. So we say this to them: 'Thank you for your concern, Grandma. I know it comes from a good place, and that you're trying to keep me safe, but this time I am going to ignore you. I don't mean to be rude, and I don't love you any less, but to make this change in my life – to go on this incredible journey of creation – I am going to need to try new things that challenge me. I do not need the safety of sticking to what I know; I need to get out there and make my mark.'

Your thoughts are well intentioned, even the ones that don't help you. Just thank them, push them out of the way, and move forward.

3. We can draw on the things we are proud of, no matter how small they seem

Even if your map is telling you that you are a bit of an underachiever, you have shown incredible strength many times in your life already. You may well have deleted all these achievements from your map, but they are still things you have done and there is no reason to believe you can't do them again. To create positive thoughts about yourself and your ability, it helps to bring these back into your awareness.

Let's try it now.

Draw eight circles on a piece of paper.

Write in each one something you have done in your life that you are even mildly proud of.

No matter how small or inconsequential your achievements may seem, make sure that you fill in all eight circles.

You can include that badge you won in the brownies and your A in General Studies. You can include anything you like, so long as you did it. It doesn't matter whether anyone else would think it's something to be proud of. This is for you.

Don't stop until you've filled all eight. It will probably get tricky at around four or five. It does for most people. Dig deep. Take your time. Get a photo album out, check your Facebook timeline, phone a friend. At all costs, get to eight!

We ask you to do this so that you remind yourself that you're amazing – that you have character, and that you can do things you've never done before. You have done many challenging things in your life already. Instead of drawing on the gaps in your experience, look back and get positive-thinking power from the things you have done.

4. We can focus on what we want rather than what we fear

Imagine waking up feeling a little anxious about a meeting you've got coming up. It's something you have to do but you've been a little nervous about since it first went in the diary.

You feel a tightness in your throat as you think about the presentation you have to make. You think about the questions you may have to face in the session – and the fact that you may not know all the answers.

You know what's going on. You kick off the duvet, swing your legs off the bed and sit up.

In your mind, you are focusing on what you fear instead of

what you want. You're building a negative picture of that meeting and it's not helping you. You call the worrying to a halt.

You've got better at spotting this. You make 'the switch'. Immediately, you stop thinking about what you're worried about and actively focus on what you *want* to happen in the meeting:

I want everyone to get on well and feel like they can explore the issues freely. I want us to be open to discussion, to ask questions and to be happy saying 'I don't know'. I want my presentation to be clear and understandable. I want to provoke a really useful conversation.

You visualize the people there smiling and enjoying the supportive dynamic in the room. You imagine how it will be as everyone leaves the meeting feeling optimistic about the project. You picture yourself driving home, feeling good about having run the session well.

You head to the bathroom, reminding yourself to have a quick read of your notes before the session, looking forward to the meeting.

Same meeting. Different thoughts. It's a mind trick – and it works.

Coaches call this 'towards' thinking. You focus on what you want rather than what you fear. It's another important method of getting your head straight.

What sort of thinking do you usually do? Do you think about what you hope will take place, what you're really excited about, what the result will be if everything goes well? Or do you find yourself focusing on what you fear, on what you want to avoid? Do you tend to think 'towards' or 'away from', or a mix of both? Take a few seconds to think about it.

There's a role for 'away from' thinking. A time when it's really useful. Contingency. What will I do if things go wrong? Special Forces troops have to do a bit of 'away from' thinking. Where are the exits? What if the door won't open? What do we do if they've moved the hostage? So do production managers: What happens if it rains? Even the Chancellor of the Exchequer has to do a bit: What happens if there is another global banking crisis? It has its place, certainly, but if it's your default setting it's worth learning to access the 'towards' version too – because a picture of what you want to happen creates energy.

Think of an event that's coming up in your calendar that you've been a little worried about. It could be something social that's been on your mind, or perhaps something to do with your work – anything at all, so long as it hasn't happened yet and you feel a small amount of concern about it.

Got one? OK. Breathe in and out deeply and steadily. Now turn your attention to your body. What subtle bodily sensations do you experience as you think about this event you're concerned about? Where in your body do you feel them? Just feel what you feel. This is going to be a useful clue for you in the future – this is where you 'feel' low-level anxiety, physically. The better you get at noticing how your body feels when you're thinking those anxious thoughts, the earlier you will be able to spot them and *switch* them.

Now – **switch your thoughts**. Switch to *towards* thinking. Actively focus your thoughts on *what you want to be the outcome* in the scenario you were thinking about. You can say it out loud if you like. What do you want that event to produce? What will it look like if it goes really well? How do you want to feel as you leave after it's been a huge success?

Notice the physical changes in your body. What do you notice now you've made this switch? You probably feel lighter, more resourceful. When you change your state like this, you can think more resourcefully about how to handle the event so it goes well.

What has changed about this event for you now? Now make a new plan. What do you want to change about your preparations?

How did you get on? Learning to control your thinking is a superpower as you make your idea happen. You can learn to notice when your thoughts are leaving you feeling unresourceful. You can switch them to *towards* thoughts. These will create energy and momentum – moving you towards what you want, rather than away from what you fear.

5. We can decide to think thoughts of outrageous success

Instead of 'I can't', try assuming 'I can' for a while. Thoughts are so powerful we can even fool our brains with outrageously positive ones. We can write a new truth and control our minds with it, just as Ken Norton did. This is how affirmations work.

Try reading this and see how you feel (say it out loud if you can):

I make ideas happen.

I create what no one has created before – persistently, and positively.

I acknowledge the voices that try to throw me off my path, and thank them for their concern, but I replace them with better, more supportive thoughts that will inspire me in my adventure.

I assume that I can do this – because I can.

I learn what I need to learn, when I need to learn it.

I support others who take the creator's path too, because I know it is a powerful experience for anyone to learn that you can do it.

I experiment and explore – and I expand.

I make this happen.

Every damn day.

Go on, say it out loud, even if you feel silly, just to prove that it works.

For extra impact, look at yourself in the mirror and say it to yourself. For extended energy, print this affirmation out and stick it on your mirror or fridge so you see it every day. Even better, write one yourself.

Whether you think you can, or you think you can't – you're right.
Henry Ford

Getting your head straight is the beginning of everything you want to do. You give yourself the best mental context for this incredible adventure that will see your idea becoming a reality. You start to notice and even control the messages your brain sends you. You access thoughts that will help you, and ditch the ones that don't.

This is more than just a chapter in a book about ideas, though. When your thinking is positive and supportive, you can imagine a future you're excited about and overcome every challenge you encounter as you head towards it. When you have your thinking helping you, you can do anything you want. Anything at all.

two
FINDING YOUR IDEA

The beginnings of all things are small. Cicero

I just started playing with materials and honestly I don't know why I did it. It was so crude – it was like kids play. It was like – get stuff, destroy it, put it back together in different ways. I played with concrete. I played with foam. I played with plaster. Seriously – random. But one day I did an experiment where I took some waste dust from the extraction system in the wood workshop and combined it with silicone sealant like people use to seal up their bath. I made these balls that looked like wood but they were balls. I just left them on the desk and went off for lunch.

I came back from lunch and they had turned into a really hard rubber. I just dropped one on the floor – and it bounced, right up to the ceiling. I just laughed and thought there's something cool in that. It sounds really nuts and there's no logic to it really but that moment just got me excited, and from there I just went on a search about what this material could be, what's its use in the world might be.

Jane ní Dhulchaointigh

When Jane ní Dhulchaointigh found her idea, it had no obvious commercial promise. It wasn't even clear what it could become. It was just a ball of goo. Yet Jane saw something in it that she wanted to explore and develop. She didn't know what it was going to be – she just knew she had to find out.

Eleven years after that moment in the workshop it's now quite clear what Jane's idea is. In fact it's become quite a big idea. Now she knows how it makes money, what it's for and why it's wonderful. She's transformed that mix of wood dust and silicone into an extraordinary product. It is now Sugru – a mouldable glue which fixes and improves practically anything. It has legions of fans, and has sold more than 5 million packs.

Jane's story is typical of the creators we met. Their ideas rarely arrived with any clarity. They arrived unformed. Instead of certainty, they simply offered an invitation to explore which the creators heeded.

It may seem obvious to say this, but we're going to say it anyway: every idea starts out *small*. In Jane's case, her idea was so small that it could hardly be called an idea. But small is how ideas begin. Small is how *everything* begins. How could it be any other way? Of course, your idea will be small and unformed when you find it. It hasn't happened yet. It's waiting to be turned into something significant – by you.

The good news is that we can all start something small. It doesn't need money, experience or expertise. It doesn't need an audience, a shop or a platform. In fact, at this stage, you only need to be bringing ideas into your life, to have the self-knowledge to know which to jump on, and to be ready to put a boatload of energy into it.

To create something significant, an unformed, unclear nugget of promise has to come into your life first. In this chapter we are going to show you how you can make sure one does, how to know it when you see it and how you can make sure it's the right ball of goo for you.

Choosing an idea to pursue is more like starting a relationship than picking a stock. You will hang out a lot, you and your idea, so finding a good one is important. Finding one you love is one of life's big moments. With the right one for you, you'll create the change in the world that you want to see. You'll enjoy the process too.

During the course of this book we're going to introduce you to a number of the creators we've met. Their ideas are finding real scale now, but they started out just like Jane did – with something they were curious about. We'll share the stories of how their ideas appeared, and how they transformed into properties which have sufficient scale to get calls from people like us wanting to write about them.

If you already have an idea you are excited about, that's good but not essential. We ask that you hold on to it lightly for the next few pages, if you can bear it. You can expect one of two things by the end of this chapter: either you'll be more committed to it than ever, or you'll want to trade it in for one you care about more.

If you don't have one you are excited about yet – just read on. Your idea – in all its early unformed glory – is waiting to be discovered. This chapter will explain what to do more of and what to do less of if you want to invite it into your life.

Feed your brain

There is nothing like looking, if you want to find something.

Bilbo Baggins, in J. R. R. Tolkien, *The Hobbit*

In the simplest sense, ideas are just small mental collisions. Thought A bumps into Thought B and the combination of these two bits of mental charge creates more energy than they had on their own. This is the alchemy of an idea.

This can only occur if you give your brain the resources it needs. It needs *stimulus* – it needs fresh Thought As and Thought Bs so it can crash them into each other. Those of us who do the same things every day: taking the same route to work, watching the same old TV shows, reading the same newspapers, having the same conversations – are failing to provide our brains with what they need. To have fresh ideas our brains need fresh stimulus: experiences, images, stories, facts, ideas, feelings which they haven't run before – so they can be used to make new connections. Fresh stimulus means fresh ideas.

Edward de Bono, the man who coined the term 'lateral think-ing', describes the mind as a mountain onto which rain is falling. Imagine so much rain falling onto it that all the raindrops are becoming rivers. This is his metaphor for how the brain organizes all the information we receive: we create 'rivers' of related information.

We organize everything we know about spaceships or basketball or crisps into a river. Whenever we need to think about any of those things – even if we're looking for something new like an idea – we head straight to our river looking for the answer.

Rivers of thinking are great if you're looking for a fact, like how close did *Rosetta* fly to Mars (250km) or what is the best-selling flavour of crisps in the UK (cheese, apparently). They're pretty good if you're looking for an opinion, like who was the greatest basketball player of all time (Michael Jordan, no question). But they are useless if you're looking for something you've never thought about before – something new in the Thought A bumps into Thought B sense. If you want a new idea for a crisp flavour and you head to your river, where all the things you know and believe about crisps and flavours are stored, you'll sit there chewing a pencil, rummaging through everything you already know – and all you'll get is thoughts you've had before.

Now look around you. Pick an item you can see. Now, using that as stimulus, come up with an idea for a crisp flavour. It might not be a very good one (you're right, carpet-flavoured crisps are just wrong), but did you notice how much easier it was to have ideas? Look again. Even better go to the fridge this time, or the spice rack, or a cookery book.

You can get systematic about this – so that you are constantly feeding your brain stimulus it can use in its day-to-day idea generation. You just need to get out into the world and try new things.

The good news is, this is fun. You now have an excellent reason to do things you don't usually do – just to feed your brain. You can hit shops you've never been in before, you can travel to new towns and countries, you can get subscriptions to magazines you've never read, buy a random book, get into a new type of music – or just surf YouTube videos of people doing things you've never seen anyone do. It's essential research to help you find your idea. You can even offset the cost against tax – so keep the receipt!

Be a maker

It's a Tuesday evening in October 2003 and Mark Zuckerberg is at his computer, with a beer. He has been dumped, so, as he often does, he is losing himself in code, creating a website. He types the following into his blog:

?phpinclude 'style.php';start_page ('Harvard Face Mash | The Process')
;print 'My mommy told me to take down this page, so it's down temporarily.';:: (0);?<font size=-110.28.03<p><i>8:13pm</i>.
<!- – Jessica Alona is a bitch. I need to think of something to make to take my mind off her.- – > I need to think of something to occupy my mind. Easy enough now I just need an idea . . .

Now. Are these the noodlings of a future internet titan, redefining even how human beings will connect with each other? Is this the critical moment when his brilliant sketches in code started to form the basis of the mighty Facebook?

No, actually. In fact this was far from his proudest moment. He later admitted: ' . . . one thing is certain, and it's that I'm a jerk for making this site'.

Mark Zuckerberg was about to make a website that every student at Harvard would want to visit, though. That night, while he struggled to get over Jessica, he was in the early stages of coding Face Mash – a 'Hot or Not'-style site that scraped photos of students from the Harvard college databases he could hack into, put them side by side, and asked the viewer to click on the one they thought was 'hottest'. Not Facebook – that would come later – Face Mash – its puerile predecessor.

But without Face Mash, there would have been no Facebook. There are structural commonalities between the two sites – but fundamentally Facebook didn't happen because of Face Mash. It happened because Mark was in the habit of making things. He was – and is – a maker, as many people who code are. If you are going to have ideas, you have to be prepared to make stuff. You have to be in the habit of it.

If Jane hadn't been playing around with waste dust and silicone, Sugru wouldn't have happened. If Mark hadn't been goofing around with his 'hot or not' site, Facebook wouldn't have happened. If he hadn't been someone who made things for fun – or to get over a girl – he wouldn't have become a billionaire just four years later.

Ideas mean nothing in the abstract. They have substance only when they are manifested in physical form. To become a creator, you have to be in the habit of making things manifest. You have to be in the habit of playing around and . . . well, creating. This is a state as much as an activity. It requires a sense of optimistic readiness, so that when you stumble across something you can do, you look at it and say, 'That would be fun! Let's give it a whirl!' You choose to be that person. To be a maker, you have to believe it's worth making stuff, even if – especially if – you don't know where it will lead, just like Mark and Jane.

By being in the habit of making, you put yourself in the way of ideas. And you will eventually create the thing that becomes something significant for you. You don't need to be a killer coder like Mark or a student of design like Jane to do this, you just need to make stuff, every day if you can, until something interesting appears.

Know what you love

What activities do you treat yourself with? What do you choose to do when you've got a couple of hours spare? What do you find yourself looking forward to a little more than the people around you?

You might love flying kites, or decorating the Christmas tree, or making bread, or playing military strategy games on your computer. It doesn't matter. In particular, it doesn't matter if it's not obvious how you would make a living out of doing that. What matters is that you notice it – because there are clues in those moments about what you love doing.

You may already have discounted something you enjoy because it isn't a 'proper' job like cabinet making, plumbing or sounding clever in meetings. You may think it's the opposite of work. But take note! The moments you lose yourself in are clues.

If you find it hard to think of moments when you lose yourself, or you simply can't get your head around the idea that they might be significant, don't be surprised – in part it's because schools inadvertently train us to ignore what we really enjoy.

At school, it's OK to get lost in algebra, French or hockey. It's OK to be fascinated by quadratic equations (anybody?), the *passé simple* or the short corner – but the student who becomes lost in doodling in an exercise book, creating worlds of dragons, orcs and mountains – unless it's during an art class – is being naughty and must learn to concentrate.

Losing yourself in something off-curriculum at school may lead to a detention, but if you're looking for an idea – losing yourself like this can be a clue of magnificent proportions.

Some people call it getting in 'the zone'. Mihály Csíkszentmihályi, one of the world's leading researchers on positive psychology, calls it 'flow'. We're not talking about a talent or a 'gift'– though that may follow because you're so happy spending time doing this activity – we're talking about it feeling so damn good solving the problem in front of you that you lose track of time. You feel perfectly challenged, seeing just enough progress from your efforts to keep you interested. It's a wonderful experience.

When have you felt this? It needn't be while you were doing something clever or fancy. Your flow will almost certainly be someone else's idea of boring. What matters is that you spot it, and you make a mental note and start to zoom out to look at what this means about what you love doing more generally.

Let's say you get a real kick out of decorating the Christmas tree. Even this apparently non-vocational (and let's face it – seasonal) pastime is a clue about what you enjoy more generally. In other words, you might not want to start a Christmas-tree decoration business (though these do exist – and imagine the holidays!), but there are clues here about what else you could do that would give you the wonderful experience of flow.

When you lose yourself in decorating a Christmas tree, you aren't just getting clues about your love of Christmas-tree decoration. You're not just finding out that you like to find a good spot to hang a bauble, or that you enjoy working out the best lines for tinsel. Zoom out a little and you'll see that you're getting clues about a much bigger picture. You're making decisions about visual impact. You're taking part in a ritual. You're designing something that others will enjoy, making something with your hands, creating something that brings the family together and combining colours and textures so that they move people. You're making a multimedia installation. If you zoom out from the simple act of decorating the tree, the worlds of design, installation, visual arts and the values of family, ritual and togetherness emerge.

Notice what you like. Our parents and teachers do their best, but no one is better at this than you. Remember – making your idea will take years. Imagine how wonderful it would be if you could be doing something you lose yourself in.

Beware of choosing an idea because it promises money or prestige

*A man is a success if he gets up in the morning and gets to bed at night,
and in between he does what he wants to do.*　　　　Bob Dylan

Viktor Frankl was a psychotherapist, active for much of the twentieth century. He created what is considered the 'Third Viennese
School of Psychotherapy' (after Freud's psychoanalysis and Adler's
individual psychology). He was an extremely insightful man.

Between 1942 and 1945 he was imprisoned in a series of
German concentration camps. In that time, his wife, mother and
brother were all murdered by Nazis.

While he was imprisoned, he did his finest work. While dealing
with the horrors of life in a concentration camp, and the loss of his
family, he developed a point of view on psychological healing so
powerful that it is practised to this day. He called it logotherapy.

As he fought to survive, he realized that even when a person
has nothing, they can feel bliss *if they can find meaning.*

His point of view offers an important lesson about success:
that money and prestige do not function as a goal. They are a
by-product.

Don't aim at success – the more you aim at it and make it a target, the more you are going to miss it. For success, like happiness, cannot be pursued; it must ensue, and it only does so as the unintended side effect of one's dedication to a cause greater than oneself or as the by-product of one's surrender to a person other than oneself . . . I want you to listen to what your conscience commands you to do, and go on to carry it out to the best of your knowledge.   Viktor Frankl

You are about to create something with your life. It will change the world. It will create a legacy. People will see what you do and they will respond to it. It will take your time and your energy and will require many decisions from you. With meaning as your North Star you will be able to endure anything as you create it.

Money and prestige are moving targets anyway. These are fluid times. Where the money comes from is changing every year and what people think is prestigious is changing too.

A survey by KPMG in 2013 of more than 900 US-based multinationals found that nine out of ten of them were expecting to change business models in the next eighteen months. They worried that what works as a business today won't necessarily bring in the dollars next year, so they're going to make big changes. Technology is changing their markets so much, that even they – huge companies in established markets – are expecting to overhaul how they make money.

You are going to need to make sure that you have reasons beyond money for making your idea happen – because the money might not arrive.

It is a risky strategy to pick an idea for prestige too. Prestige is also a moving target. Like fashion, it is fickle in the extreme. It's wise not to rely on other people for motivation, because they rarely give you what you want.

First, you will have to work hard on your idea for quite some time before it starts to inspire any awe in others. Even then, in the experience of many of the creators we met, people's responses to your idea will be more complex than you expect.

You can expect to receive negativity as much as praise as you and your idea start to become visible to people you've never met before, no matter how noble your intent. As your idea breaks through and becomes something that people have an opinion about, you will inspire trolls as much as plaudits.

Some people will be impressed and want to give you love for what you are achieving. Others will wish that they were making *their* idea happen, and feel envious of you. Others – family and friends in particular – might wish you had stayed the same as you were, instead of making this significant change in your life.

So forget prestige. People are hard to please and impossible to second-guess anyway. You're better off just focusing on enjoying doing something – anything – well.

Prestige is like a powerful magnet that warps even your own beliefs about what you enjoy.   Paul Graham

Paul Graham's company, Y Combinator, has funded some of the most successful start-ups of the modern tech era. His view is, 'If you do anything well enough, you make it prestigious.' Each of his businesses is a masterclass in doing things well. Take a look at some of the projects he is involved with:

- Airbnb – the company has enabled millions of people to stay in other people's homes anywhere in the world for the night. Now valued at $20bn (**http://www.wsj.com/articles/the-secret-math-of-airbnbs-24-billion-valuation-1434568517**), it is essentially a home rental site, done very well.
- Dropbox – valued at $10bn, it is basically a way of saving files, done well.
- Reddit – online forums (done well) with a natty up-voting system. It has a valuation upward of $500 million and is currently one of the fifty most visited websites in the world.

Airbnb, Dropbox and Reddit are among the most prestigious businesses around. Twenty years ago, it was prestigious to be a banker. These days it's prestigious to build a tech company, be a TV chef or be in One Direction. What's going to be prestigious next year is

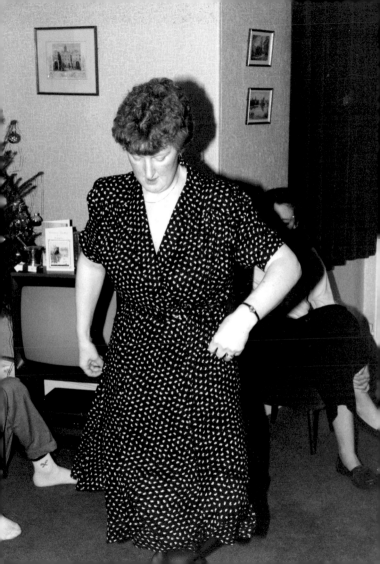

impossible to guess. Find something you're excited to develop, that has meaning for you, and do it well. Money and prestige will follow.

Forget being original

What has been will be again, what has been done will be done again; there is nothing new under the sun.   Ecclesiastes 1:9

'It's not original' is the most careless of criticisms. It says nothing more than 'I've seen something like this before'. It forgets that everything has its roots in everything that came before it – and it undervalues the energy and will it takes to create *anything*.

The urge to make something is a precious energy. If you ever feel it, make the most of it. Even if there are elements of your idea that are visible in other ideas, grab the opportunity to create with both hands.

The history of ideas is a tapestry of interconnecting ideas, with one idea inspiring the next. Everything is connected. Your idea might build on a concept from eighteenth-century France. Someone may have opened one of those a few years back on the High Street. Or it could be a straight copy of something that went massive in California in the sixties. As long as you respect intellectual property laws, it doesn't matter. If you insist on 100 per cent originality in your idea you will be searching for a very, very long time because nothing is entirely original. Just find something you are excited to do – and get started.

What will make your idea truly original is *how* you do it. Your idea is the ultimate arena for you to find your voice, and create something representative of the change you want to see in the world. You make something original by being yourself (we'll get into this a lot more later).

When we started writing this book, someone we admire told us he thought 'the concept wasn't particularly fresh'. We thought of all the thousands of books about innovation, ideas, creativity and business and we started to wonder whether we actually have anything new to offer. Everywhere we looked we saw other people's ideas that were connected to what we were trying to do. We tend to think that we're pretty resilient when it comes to getting on and doing things, but we started to worry that he was right.

Thinking like that never helped anyone. It's how two optimistic, hopeful people like us were taken down, briefly: by lazy criticism. We got over ourselves in the end and returned to the one thing we were certain about – that we wanted to write this book. We focused on the reason we wanted to do it; its *meaning* for us: that we want to share what we've learned with other people so that they might get the pleasure of making their ideas happen.

Debating whether something is original is pretty much the definition of wasting time. There is no objective truth, and it doesn't take you anywhere good knowing either way. We still don't know if this book is original – but what we do know is that it is the book we wanted to write, so we've done it. We got on with what we wanted to do – the idea that is right for us.

We hope that the idea that is right for *you* is starting to reveal itself. If you're not clear on what you want to do exactly, don't worry. Keep feeding your brain, learn what you care about and lose yourself in, set your goal as seeking meaning and your idea will appear in time.

Creator stories

Every idea has a story. Knowing how another creator found their idea and how they developed it helps us learn about where our own ideas will come from and how we might pursue ours.

We have already met Jane and her idea Sugru. To feed your brain a little more, we are going to introduce a good range of creators throughout this book. We'll share the stories of their ideas, and in particular how they found them. Here's the first.

Creator story 1: Solving the problem in your passion – Kennedy City Bicycles

James Kennedy was a keen cyclist working in trend forecasting. He had wanted to start his own business for some years: a café and even a cinema were some of his early daydreams. Then one day in January 2011, when he was buying a bike for himself, he realized what he wanted to do.

Everywhere he looked for a custom bike, the prices were high and the ranges too complex.

'I looked into how much the parts were, and realized if I offered a small number of options I would be able to make great custom bikes affordably. When I realized I could do it better and for less than other people, I felt almost obliged to do it – for people like me who wanted their own unique bike but couldn't afford to pay a small fortune.'

He had found the problem in his passion – and he decided to solve it. Before a year had passed, James was able to offer a beautifully designed, handmade, bespoke single-speed bike for £450, delivered in a week. Kennedy City Bicycles was born.

Working in an area you have passion for and solving a problem you believe needs solving is a powerful mix. James is relatively new in town, but he's showing how things can be done better. He's on a mission.

Have faith in your ability. More often than not, when you try something new, particularly if it is an informed decision, you will probably succeed and things will go well as opposed to badly. We have that fear of the unknown, but I've found that you can get over that cognitive bias. There is that assumption in all of us that what we don't know is scary – that tiger in the trees. But just by beating it into yourself every day that unknown and scary things can be good for you, you can achieve amazing things.

James Kennedy

· how to find an idea like james did ·

Look out for the conventions you can break
James found a convention in the bike market – that bikes are either off the shelf and identical or completely bespoke. He decided instead to offer three different frames, three different handlebars and three different colours. He knew this was enough personalization

continued

for most people, and it meant James's product has stayed relatively simple and affordable.

Solve a problem and you will find a market
If you feel frustrated by your experience in a certain category, you can be pretty sure there will be other people who do too. Take your frustration as the evidence that there is an unmet need – it will show up sooner or later in other people.

Find fellow crusaders
Once you think you have identified the problem you want to solve, speak to other people who feel the same way. Explore their logic about the problem and work out how you can solve it.

Stay a fan
The strength of this being your passion is that you are your future customer. You experience the problem that needs solving. If you are personally experiencing a shortcoming in any category then you can solve it to your own satisfaction. Stay involved in your passion and you'll develop an instinctive feel for the right solutions.

You'll read more about James and many other creators in this book and at theideainyou.com. For now, we want to return the focus to you and your idea.

three

LANDING YOUR IDEA

Everyone who's ever taken a shower has an idea. It's the person who gets out of the shower, dries off and does something about it who makes the difference.

Nolan Bushnell, founder of Atari and
Chuck E. Cheese's Pizza-Time Theatres chain

By now, we hope you are starting to build a belief that you can find an idea and make it happen. Perhaps you are also homing in on one you're excited about too. If you don't have an idea yet, just read on. In time, if you follow the advice so far, an idea you love will arrive.

Whatever your idea, if it is nothing more than a conversation down the pub or a dream in your mind, its wheels are just spinning. It can't go anywhere. You need to get it out of your head – so you can get on and do it. You do this by writing it down. This may seem simple, but it is critical. By writing your idea down, you make the rubber hit the road.

We call this 'landing the idea'. Once your idea is out of your head and onto a piece of paper (we prefer paper to pixels on a screen), you can have a proper look at it and get to work on it.

Until we 'land' them, ideas tend to float around in our heads as a collection of thoughts, feelings and images. They stay subjective and change from one day to the next. An idea in *your* mind can be quite different from the same one in someone else's. There is scope for confusion.

Commit an idea to words on paper, though, and it stops moving around. You gain access to its working parts too, so you can start to decide how to make it succeed.

But first, what is an idea? We've used the word quite loosely so far in this book. Now we need to get specific. It is about to get really important.

From here on, this is how we're defining an idea: as *something you can do*.

It needn't be easy to do, or immediately obvious how *you* will do it – but when you write an idea down, it must be explaining something that someone can get on and do. Here's an example:

Some people might say that 'Put a man on the moon' was one of the biggest ideas of the second half of the twentieth century. Being sticklers for this kind of thing (as we hope you are becoming), we would say no – that is not yet an idea.

Here's an idea: *The Apollo programme. Give NASA the funds necessary, and the political support the programme needs to build the required skills and technology to put a man on the moon by the end of the sixties.*

Can you see the difference? 'Put a man on the moon' is more of a goal than an idea. It's not something you can go off and do yet. Instead of an idea, we'd call 'Put a man on the moon' a *thought*. The thought is the idea's lesser cousin, and the thing people most often confuse with an idea. Here are some more thoughts masquerading as ideas:

- A revolutionary new app which makes you happier day by day.
- The easiest way to get fit using your own body weight.
- A way of getting to school which is safer than walking but less costly than public transport.
- A new type of political party that listens to what people really want.

Thought. Thought. Thought. Thought!

Look back through them – even though they look like 'good

ideas' they are in fact all problems that still need solving. Just looking at them makes us scream 'HOW?'

Here's another thought: 'A business which gets people break-dancing as a form of exercise'.

This sounds like an interesting idea for a business (especially if you like breakdancing and exercise), but it's not – yet – an idea. We still don't know what this business does. We need to go through the process of asking 'how?' That way we'll find lots of ways of delivering on the promise of that thought – and we'll know what to go and do. Here are some ideas which turn that thought into something you can do:

* BreakFit – a weekly class at the local gym mixing breakdancing and fitness.
* A 1hr DVD – *Get Fit the BreakFit Way*.
* A channel on YouTube featuring BreakFit training videos.

One final example of a thought for us to focus on:

* Get everyone in the office to eat healthier food. Just as for 'Put a man on the moon', this looks like a 'good idea' but we still need to answer the question HOW? before we know what to do. It's still a thought. It is a problem that still needs solving. What could we do?

We could hire a chef to cook a lovely healthy lunch for us every day, or run No Fry Up February, or swap our biscuits for nuts and raisins. In fact, the list of ideas we could have against the *thought* 'Get everyone in the office to eat healthier food' is endless.

Remember, turning your thought into an idea is essential for you as a creator because it means you can start doing – and that is the only way you move the game on. There is nothing wrong with having goals or wishes, but until you turn them into something you can do, your wheels are spinning.

Here is **an idea** against that thought about getting everyone in the office to eat healthier food:

* Fruit Bowl Mondays: Put a bowl on everyone's desk and fill it up with fresh fruit every Monday morning.

Whether we like the idea or not (our hunch is that we could improve the name!), 'Fruit Bowl Mondays' is ready to do. It's so clear that even someone who wasn't there when we came up with the idea could get on and do it if they wanted to. They would need to work out some operational detail (like where to get the bowls and the fruit, and what kind of fruit to get, and how much to spend) but the basic structure of the idea is in place.

Leaving aside whether Fruit Bowl Mondays is an original or inspiring idea (be nice, please!), you will see how – now it's an idea – it creates momentum. Now, we know what to do. This is the first stage of the process of landing your idea – double-checking that you have an idea at all. Making sure that you have *something you can do*.

· DO IT NOW ·

If you have an idea, double-check it's an idea and not a thought. Transform it into something you can do by asking **how** it might be done.

Don't worry if you're not sure exactly how to do it yourself yet, just make sure that it is an idea and not a thought.

Creator story 2: Have fun making stuff – Mallow and Marsh

Harriot Pleydell-Bouverie started Mallow and Marsh, a gourmet marsh-mallow company, in 2013. The idea came to her after a bet in the pub.

'I already had a jewellery business that I had launched, really because I thought it was a commercial opportunity, but it wasn't really working. I was on a training course and, over a few drinks at the end of the day, the group got to discussing marshmallows – and whether you could make them at home. It all turned into a challenge. I was up until the early hours that night making my first ever batch of marshmallows. I loved doing it but the best thing was watching the joy people got from eating them. In less than ten

hours I got more people talking about my marshmallows than I'd ever seen talking about my jewellery business. I knew I was on to something.'

Ideas really can come from anywhere but you have to make them. As we saw earlier, one of the best ways of finding your idea is by being in the habit of making things. Eventually you'll make something that will have a peculiar and powerful energy.

'We spent hours hand-whisking and making our first ever marshmallows. We made blue ones and bacon ones and all sorts – and brought them in the next day. I was amazed – people loved them.'

Harriot was aware enough to realize that the fun that she had making her marshmallows, and the enjoyment of those whom she shared them with, and the fact that everyone was amazed that she could make something overnight – added up to something promising. It contained enough positive energy for the germ of her great idea to grow. She was also then brave enough to listen to her feelings and take the leap.

· how to do what harriot did ·

Try things

Every experience you get is an opportunity to learn, and to create. When you get the opportunity to try something you haven't done before, why not take it? Harriot's conversation about marshmallows in the pub would have gone nowhere if she'd just gone to bed when she got home from the pub. Instead she started experimenting *straight away*. Now she runs one of the fastest-growing food businesses in the UK.

Know what good enough looks like

She asked us not to mention this, but we think it shows how resourceful Harriot is: she used a rubber glove as the mould for her first ever marshmallows. These were the opening moments of Britain's finest gourmet marshmallow company, but a humble rubber glove was enough for its first ever batch. Harriot sensed that she needed momentum more than perfection that night, and got the job done. Of course, Mallow and Marsh use the finest moulds available now.

Find out more about Harriot's story at theideainyou.com.

Writing down your idea

When you write down an idea, you impose some clarity on it. It's a critical act because it removes doubt. It doesn't ask you to commit to an idea exactly – you can still change it whenever you like – but you will stop it wriggling around and changing form for long enough to get to grips with what you've got.

We are going to share with you now how the professionals do this. It's a way to capture ideas created for one of the harshest environments for innovation: the focus group.

Imagine a roomful of people sitting in a circle. There are comfortable leather chairs, a couple of pot plants and a nice selection of biscuits. Executives watch from behind a one-way mirror, occasionally checking their emails. Back in the main room, a moderator is holding up a board with text and pictures on it, asking questions. He's trying to find out what the people in the circle, the 'consumers' (as these human beings recruited based on their demographics and buying habits are known), think of a new product.

In that situation, more often than not, the text on that board will take the form of a 'concept' – an idea, written down. The 'concept' is one of the key tools of the innovation consultant. It is the quickest and most helpful way of summarizing an idea in its early stages.

As an example, here's a concept we've prepared for the (quite brilliant) idea, Fruit Bowl Mondays:

Fruit Bowl Mondays

The thing about healthy food is that you only tend to eat it when it's right in front of you.

Introducing Fruit Bowl Mondays – a new easy and healthy option for the whole office: a fruit bowl on your desk, filled to the brim with delicious fruit every Monday morning.

Fruit Bowl Mondays – healthy food at your desk.

It is a big moment for any idea when you write it as a concept. Once you have your idea in concept form, it is somehow alive. You can now look at it, and this makes life much easier.

The concept is the blueprint for your idea. It reveals the four core elements in any idea too so you can examine them and improve them:

1. What your idea is called.
2. The need it meets for people.
3. How it works, in basic terms.
4. The benefits people get from using it.

If you break your idea down into these four core elements, you can look at them one at a time. This is why the concept is such an important tool – it forces you to think about the key drivers for the success of an idea. You can't ignore them – they're in front of you now in black and white.

Before we look at each of the four core elements in the concept in detail, we'll share one final example concept. Do you remember the location-based reminder idea we mentioned in the introduction? We decided in the end that it wasn't the right idea for us to pursue – because we didn't want to spend the next few years doing it, but we did a little bit of work on it first, to work out whether the idea had legs. Here's the concept we wrote for it:

MemoryJogger

There are times when your diary can't help you to remember something, because what matters is **where** you are rather than **when** something is happening. Say you need to remember bin bags at the supermarket, or to say something important to someone when you're round at their house, or to pick up some kindling at the petrol station – your diary can't help you because you only know **where** you will be when you need to remember and not **when** that will be.

MemoryJogger solves this problem. It is a new location-based reminder app for your phone. It links a message to a GPS location, so you get a reminder *where* you need it – in the supermarket, round at your friend's house, or at the petrol station.

Just 'pin' a note to a location on the map, and the next time you go there, MemoryJogger will ping up a reminder on your screen – and you'll get the reminder you need.

MemoryJogger – a reminder where you need it most.

Can you see how in concept form it feels much more real? It still wasn't coded or prototyped in any way, but we were able to look closely at it and we could start to sharpen it or decide to leave it and focus on something else.

The elements in a concept

We are going to share more about the four core elements in a concept now. Use this example concept and how we explain the different parts as a springboard for thinking about your own idea, if you have one. Consider what the elements of your concept should be – and get ready to write it. (Again – don't worry if you don't have an idea yet. Just read on.)

1. The headline – what you're calling your idea
Giving your idea a **headline** – for example MemoryJogger – gives it energy, and makes it feel real, even before it is real. At concept stage, this is a working title. In time, as you explore URLs and trademarking and branding, you might want to or have to change your name. For now this is a label that allows you to identify it, making it easy to talk about, and will create some energy around it. As a name, MemoryJogger has a lot more energy than 'The Location Based Reminder Idea' – we decided that it would do for now.

2. The need
We call the **need** the 'nodding factor' because a good one gets people nodding in agreement with you.

Imagine a potential customer of your idea sitting in front of you. If you've got this bit of your concept right, they'll smile and nod and say, 'I know exactly what you mean. That is so true for me too!' If you're getting nodding, you're on to something.

> There are times when your diary can't help you to remember something, because what matters is where you are rather than when something is happening. Say you need to remember bin bags at the supermarket, or to say something important to someone when you're round at their house, or to pick up some kindling at the petrol station – the diary can't help you because you only know **where** you will be when you need to remember and not **when** that will be.

The interesting thing about working through the need in any idea is that it is right at the heart of its potential. It forces us to ask the fundamental question: what is the problem people have that our idea solves? Why does our idea have to exist? Without a need that gets people nodding, it's likely that your idea won't be required or valued.

Now, when we look at the MemoryJogger concept, we wonder whether anyone really suffers from the problem it suggests it can solve. It may be true that diaries can't help you remember something which isn't time-based, but is this really a big hole in anyone's life? It was for the person who'd forgotten the bin bags in our story, but will enough people in the world have the same problem? We're not sure.

If we were planning to create MemoryJogger, this is something we would make sure we found out more about – and get to a positive point of view on – before we spent time and energy developing it.

3. The process: how it works

The **process** is the part of your concept that addresses the question any sensible buyer would ask: how does it work? This is where you explain to your imaginary buyer *how* this idea will deliver brilliantly against the need they were nodding about.

> MemoryJogger is a new location-based reminder app for your phone. It links a message to a GPS location, so you get a

reminder **where** you need it – in the supermarket, round at your friend's house, or at the petrol station.

Just 'pin' a note to a location on the map, and the next time you go there, MemoryJogger will ping up a reminder on your screen – and you'll get the reminder you need.

This bit of the concept explains the process in basic terms. We're not designing the detail of the product here; we're just having a first go at describing specifically what the user experiences. To get to this detail all we did was ask ourselves the questions a potential buyer would ask. 'What's the process for setting up a reminder? What happens to actually remind you? How does the damn thing work?'

In the early stages of the MemoryJogger idea it doesn't particularly matter whether we know technically how that reminder will be displayed, what code we need to write, or how we get a pin on a map. That is something we will work on later. What matters here is that we have identified roughly how it works (we're hunching – more on that later) and have had a go at expressing it – so we can look at it in our concept.

The outcome we want from this element of our concept is for us to have done the thinking about how the idea will work in general terms. We may also want to show it to our potential customer. Ideally our description will help them understand what it does, reassure them that the idea will work and help them believe that it will deliver against the need they have (the one they were nodding about). Again, we've written what we believe is needed (and no more) to make these things happen.

4. The benefit
What is the **benefit** of your idea? How does it improve a user's day? What are you offering that they will be pleased to experience?

The benefit in your concept is your in-a-nutshell version of why your idea is brilliant. It will be useful whenever you speak to someone. Even if you have only ten seconds, you'll be able to sell them on the power of your idea. It gives a lift to your concept at the end – sending the user off into a reverie about how much it will improve their lives.

MemoryJogger – a reminder where you need it most.
Fruit Bowl Mondays – healthy food at your desk.

At the beginning of the concept you set up your need. Your benefit finishes your concept with confirmation that your product does indeed deliver against that need. It provides a reassuring lift at the end.

We like to imagine the benefit as being a bit like the strapline in an ad. The benefit sells your idea. We might even have some fun and inject a bit of energy into the benefit element. Let's pump their tyres a bit:

MemoryJogger – reminds you there, there and there.
Fruit Bowl Mondays – putting healthy on our desks.

You absolutely can have fun with words to give your concept loads of energy. Whatever happens, though, make sure not to do this at the expense of clarity. Writing a concept is a way of organizing your thinking, so make sure it leaves it feeling organized!

And remember, this is just for now. Over time, your idea will evolve, and so will your concept. Getting it written is more important than getting it right. You're having a good play with your idea to see whether it works and if it's what you want to do.

So, to recap, these are the elements of the all-important concept. If you've got an idea, you're going to write one of these in a moment, so please watch carefully:

1. Headline: a name that captures the energy of your idea, and one that you like and will be happy saying a lot.
2. Need: the need your idea will meet. This bit will get your user nodding and saying, 'Yes – I have that problem. Help me!'
3. Process: product detail and reasons to believe. What your product does and how it works, clearly presented so that even a sceptic will see it will meet the need.
4. Benefit: how your idea will change the user's life for the better, expressed directly to the buyer, with some energy!

What's the point of a concept?

Your concept is more than just a good way of looking at your idea before it exists. It's a lens to look at your idea through once you're underway too. Writing a concept makes you answer the key questions we all need to have a point of view on as we develop our ideas: what they're called, what problem they solve, how they do it, and why that's great for the customer. In the busy-ness of bringing your idea to life, getting back to what your concept is, is a good way of taking a few minutes to make sure all your action is pointing in the right direction – like pulling a compass out of a bag on a long walk so you can check you're on the right path.

> ## · DO IT NOW ·
> ## write a quick concept for your idea
>
> If your idea is even vaguely clear in your mind – write a concept for it.
>
> Note – 'Get it written, don't get it right!' is what we tend to say at this stage. Absolutely don't get bogged down in this. Write a quick version. Your idea will evolve over time anyway. You can turn to your concept whenever you like – and write it as an exercise to get clarity about your idea and what to do.
>
> Remember – your concept is based on your current hunches – about what it should be called, the need it will meet for people, about how it works so that people believe in it (the process: product detail and reason(s) to believe) and about what the idea will offer them (the benefit).
>
> If you're wondering whether you can be bothered, we understand. But remember, this is moving the game on – even in five minutes you will transform how you think about your idea.
>
> And if you still have no clue what your idea is, don't worry – just go straight to the next chapter.
>
> You can download a free idea concept template from theideainyou.com.

Making a Start

four

STARTING

The Hero's Journey is one of literature's most common plot devices. Many of our most famous stories follow its arc: *Star Wars, The Lord of the Rings*, Harry Potter, *Raiders of the Lost Ark* and *Finding Nemo* among many others.

Like Luke, Frodo, Harry, Indiana and Nemo, you are a normal person (or halfling, or clown fish) setting off on an extraordinary journey:

We meet you in everyday life.

Life is good enough – but you can sense there is a challenge coming which will change your life for ever.

Something happens to you, and you sense that you are being invited to go on a journey. Do you heed the call to adventure?

At first you refuse to leave. It's not the right time. You get stuck back in the monotony of everyday life.

This can't continue for ever, though – you know you will have to go eventually. The journey won't leave you alone. It is everywhere you look. And you know you are slowly dying, staying here.

A helper arrives. They build in you the belief that you can indeed make the journey. You feel safe enough to trust them to lead you to the point of no return.

You cross the threshold. Now you can't turn back. No longer surrounded by the familiar structures of home, you start to feel exposed to the dangers of a new world.

Your transformation begins. You are tested but you discover a benign energy all around you that you can call on for help. Partial victories reveal glimpses of the future you seek, but the journey continues.

Temptation. A brush with what impresses you most reminds you that you are flawed – but this time your ability to push past the temptation reminds you of the purity of your purpose.

The big moment. Atonement. You face down your greatest fear – that which holds the most power over you. This must be beaten if you are to be truly free. And so in a triumphant battle, you overcome it.

Reward. You get what you are looking for and then rest.

Return. You return home to celebrate and pass on the elixir of your teaching. You are tested once more, on the way home, as if to show you what you have learned.

Is it grandiose to suggest that the experience of making the idea in you happen will be like Frodo's or Nemo's epic journeys? We'll see. You are embarking on possibly the most intense journey of your life. The challenges you face will reveal hidden truths about yourself and the world.

The Hero's Journey is in so many stories because it resonates with us. It meets with our own understanding of what it takes to achieve greatness. It helps us understand change too: it shows a transition, from an ordinary life to an extraordinary one – from Tatooine to the Death Star, from the Shire to Mordor – from your life now to the one with an idea changing the world in it.

The point of your Hero's Journey is not you getting your idea listed in Walmart, or being on TV, or buying a big house in the Bahamas, or even you showing those idiots at school that you did something with your life. The point of this journey is the impact it will have on you.

The real story in *The Lord of the Rings* is Frodo – and how he grows in the face of the many challenges he faces. The real story in *Star Wars Episode 4* isn't the destruction of the Death Star, it's the transformation of Luke, a young moisture farmer from Tatooine, into a Jedi knight.

This journey you are about to set out on might look like the journey of your idea – but it's really your journey. Like Luke and

Frodo, you will be tested – many times. You will have to change direction from time to time. You may even have to cut your losses. But the one constant, and arguably the real goal, is your own development. You will learn what's possible, and you will surpass it. You will learn how powerful you are. This is the Hero's Journey.

How to find your inner Baggins

'I will take the Ring,' he said, 'though I do not know the way.'
Frodo Baggins, in J. R. R. Tolkien, *The Fellowship of the Ring*

One of the most famous journeys in literature is taken by Frodo Baggins, a small halfling with wide eyes, furry feet and a love of ale and breakfast. In *The Lord of the Rings*, the young hobbit sets out on a journey full of uncertainty and danger. What makes him one of literature's greatest heroes is that he commits to the journey *despite not knowing where it will lead.*

This is the same for everyone: whether you are a young Padawan, halfling, half-blood prince, a little clown fish, or just a humble creator, the journey has to begin, even though – and perhaps *because* – you don't know where it will lead.

In the story of any idea, the ordinary person who commits to the journey has more chance of success than the extraordinary person who only half-commits. You cannot expect to dot every i, or cross every t before you go – this is procrastination in everything but name. You have to set out even though you are not completely ready, and even though you cannot be sure how things are going to turn out – because once you are on the road, everything changes.

There is a story inside Nike about how its now legendary strapline – Just Do It – was created. Back in 1988, the advertising team were discussing options. Their best shot at that point was 'Do It!' The people around the table liked it somewhat, but they knew it was missing something.

Legend has it that Dan Wieden, one of the founders of the advertising agency with the Nike account, put the word 'just' in front of it.* The team all spotted the special resonance of the word 'just' in that context. It adds insight to the words – it reflects a truth about how human beings often are in the face of challenges.

On the whole we tend to do things when we know what will happen. Like the child on the diving board, we work through potential outcomes and estimate how safe we are before we make a decision. We check the angles, thinking about how things will turn out – sometimes to such a degree that the moment passes. The line 'Just Do It' has struck a chord with generations because it says, in effect, 'Do it, *even though* you don't know what will happen if you do.' It is a leap of faith.

You might be uncertain what your idea will become, or even where you should start – these will come later – but you will need a fire in your belly. So before you venture any further, before you step out of that little round door, and place your hairy Halfling foot onto the cobbles outside, do the thing you have to do before any of this can happen. Commit to your journey. Whatever it holds.

· DO IT NOW ·
commit to your journey

Just do it! Even though you don't know where it will lead. Commit to your journey. Write it in the box below or on a scrap of paper, wherever you want. But turn that thought into form. Make it real, so you can look back on this as a moment of significance in your life. The moment you reached the point of no return. DO IT NOW. Stick it on the fridge – so that it winks at you every time you pass through the kitchen.

Even though I don't know where I am going, I commit to the journey of making my idea happen.
Signed: . . . .

---

* His initial inspiration, in fact, came from the final words of Gary Gilmore, a murderer executed by firing squad in Utah in 1977, but Nike don't talk about this so much.

Managing some expectations

First, we want to dash the Myth of Overnight Success.

It's exciting to imagine that our lives could change overnight, that we might find huge success suddenly, like picking the right lottery numbers.

Since the internet emerged as the ultimate sharing device, it has looked like there is a new shape to success. These days videos 'go viral', music tracks 'blow up' and fads go worldwide in weeks. It can seem like all you need to do is have an idea, brand it and share it, and then play the waiting game. It's tempting to imagine that the internet will do the work, sending your idea around the world to millions before bringing back fame, wealth and prestige.

It may seem cheap to tell you this now – after we've asked you to commit to the journey – but we thought we might put you off if we told you sooner: this isn't going to happen quickly.

I had the idea for Sugru eleven years ago when I was still a Product Design student. It was after eight years that we went live with the product you see today. And then everyone started saying we were an overnight success! So yeah, I guess it took us eight years to be an overnight success!

Jane ní Dhulchaointigh, Sugru

Here's why people think success happens overnight.

We tend to hear about ideas once they are getting very successful. We assume – since we hadn't heard of the idea before – that it must have happened suddenly. We don't hear about it while it's being worked on, about the prototypes and revisions, or the dark nights of the soul when the creator considered jacking it all in because it wasn't working as they'd hoped. We don't hear about the millions of other ideas that are well underway but still months or years from breaking through.

Ideas become successful only when their creator is persistent. You have to stay in the game. You have to create change in the world for a sustained period if you want your idea to reach a large number of people. This stuff does not happen overnight. It takes time. We weren't using the term Hero's Journey lightly.

It's important to know that making your idea happen isn't just a grand gesture: you have an idea, the world finds out about it and then you live happily ever after. No, it's a journey with a million steps in it.

If all this talk about how much effort is involved is putting you off, it might not be a bad thing. We hope you'll be back when you really do have the fire in your belly.

Because of the amount of energy required to make an idea happen, day in, day out for years, creators need something almost delusional about them as they set out on this journey. A fervour, which to some looks like madness. Like Frodo in the shadow of Mount Doom, you won't know what is going to happen or what you will learn from your journey, you just know you have to keep going.

Crushing the fear of failure

To avoid criticism, do nothing, say nothing, be nothing.

Elbert Hubbard

Any fear you have of falling on your face and looking like a fool as you show your idea to the world is completely natural. It's in your DNA. In our primeval past, staying popular with the tribe was essential for survival. Losing their support would put you at risk of being cast out, into the wilderness. In the days of sabretooth tigers it made sense to keep your head down and resist trying anything that the group might think was a bit fancy. It's not so important now, but our instincts still warn us about it.

Our instincts want us to stay right where we are, where survival is guaranteed: on the sofa, eating HobNobs, quietly avoiding being cast out by the group, doing nothing much with our lives. As Antony Robbins, a behemoth in the world of motivational speaking, puts it, *'Most of the things that are valuable in our lives require us to go against the basic conditioning of our nervous systems.'* It feels somehow unsafe to expose ourselves to judgement from the rest of society.

The good news is that your fear of rejection will reduce over time, in proportion to how far and how often you put yourself out there. When you feel that rush of fear as you put your point of view, your art, or your idea out into the world, this is not an invitation to step back into the shadows; it's a sign that you are at the edge, right where you should be, exploring how things might be. Those sensations are a sign that you are in good working order, that your human instincts are alive and well, and also that amazing things are about to happen. Turning back now is exactly the wrong thing to do.

There will be a key moment when fear will be at its strongest – when you hit 'send' on the invitations to your event, or you flip the sign on the door from CLOSED to OPEN for the first time, or when you upload your first video, or seal the first package of products for the retailer, or send your big press release, or whatever it is that sees you finally putting your idea in front of the world. Enjoy the ride; notice how you react. Feel the rush and move forward. You are not going to be expelled from the tribe or sent out into the bush. You're safe. In fact, any fear of failure you are feeling is about to take more of a kicking in one day than it ever has before.

Just to burst the bubble on your fear of failure once and for all, know that the most common response to your idea in the early days will be indifference. People won't laugh or tell you how ridiculous your idea is, any more than they'll run around telling their friends how amazing you are, they'll just go about their business. You will be excited about what you're doing, so it looms huge in your mind, but even in your friends' and families' heads this is just a new project you've started working on. They haven't done all the thinking you've done. They don't have the same mental picture of the future, of the house by the sea, of the TV interviews as you launch your third New York store. They're getting on with their lives, like everyone else.

But what can you do to overcome the fear of failure? How can you find a way to summon the courage to put your original work out into the world? How can you overcome the instinct any sane person has, to care about what the rest of the tribe thinks?

Well, one easy way is to find a new tribe.

Your new tribe is everyone else who is bravely making things happen – creators like you. People who understand the journey you are on and will want to help you.

To join this tribe you don't need to leave your current ones – your family, your friends or your football team. You just add this to your collection. The tribe of creators is easy to connect with: through social media and blogs. You can find them on websites about making things happen like Etsy, Kickstarter, Udemy and Medium. You can meet other creators through the free Creator Community at theideainyou.com.

Here's how the tribe of creators works, in our experience:

- They are active in their support of other creators – they know what it's like.
- They are generous in their praise of those who are going through the tricky process of putting themselves and their ideas out into the world.
- They are authentic – they say what they believe.
- They are respectful of differences of opinion.
- They help other creators when they can.
- They are delighted when good things happen to others and supportive when things get tough for them.
- They are happy to share what they have learned.

Creator story 3: Go on an adventure – Pizza Pilgrims

Thom and James Elliot didn't analyse a market or write a business plan to find their idea. They went on an adventure.

They decided to buy a three-wheeled van with a pizza oven built into the back and drove it from the heel of Italy all the way back to London. They set out with an open mind and a hunger for adventure, and developed a passion for Neapolitan pizza, and a network of experts and suppliers, on the way home.

They had the presence of mind to tell a few TV production companies about their plan, and one sent a crew on their adventure with them.

Thom and James's adventure was the beginning of one of the UK's fastest growing restaurant concepts, Pizza Pilgrims. As Thom says:

'We didn't set out to create lots of restaurants. At best, we thought James might be able to sell pizzas at events when we got back. I was expecting to have to get a job when I got home. But our journey started in motion a series of events that led us to where we are today.'

· how to do what thom and james did ·

Have a goal

What distinguishes an adventure like this from a holiday is that you have an objective beyond having fun. What you do obviously depends on what you care about – you might want to meet everyone with the same name as you, or chronicle the finest cheese makers in the north of England, or connect two professors whose work you admire. James and Thom wanted to learn how to make pizzas Napoli-style. Whatever your interest is, by committing to a goal you give your adventure purpose. By immersing yourself in a topic you're interested in you will spot opportunities, and learn where your passion lies.

Capture content, build a brand

Adventures are powerful fuel for an idea – they create a ready-made brand with a mission and a backstory. They also generate excellent content. Produce a book, a blog or even a film of your experiences. Get people following you while you're out there. Thom and James's adventure created the ultimate content – a broadcast TV show.

Take a partner

It is more fun going on an adventure with a friend. You'll laugh more, meet more people and create better relationships if you are having a great time. It's also useful – you can discuss what you're discovering on your adventure and plan what you want to do with it when you get home.

Find out more about Thom and James at theideainyou.com.

Haters gonna hate

It is important to know that your idea will be rejected by some people. It does hurt to be told your idea sucks but it's just part of sharing your idea with the world. People will offer their opinions on it and some of them will be negative. You only have to look at the reviews on Amazon of any bestseller: there is always the full range, from five-star to one-star reviews. There is no accounting for taste. Often, it's not you or, indeed, your idea. It's them.

In popular culture, there is a bit of a thing for hating these days, and you might find yourself on the receiving end of it when you stick your head above the parapet and share your idea with the world. *Star Magazine*, a US celebrity gossip mag, even does an annual poll of 'Most Hated Celebrities' (winner 2014: Gwyneth Paltrow). It also has a section called 'Worst of the Week' showing 'fashion disasters'. It seems the more you do, and the more visibly you do it, the more comfortable people feel rejecting you.

Even hater-grade feedback on your idea can lead somewhere good, even if it's only for the hater. If you can resist the temptation to retaliate, you can certainly help them see that being unpleasant to someone who is putting their life and soul into an idea is a ridiculous thing to do. This is a service to all creators, and it may help them realize that they too could create something useful someday.

Hater: *This is sh*t.*
Creator: *Thanks for your feedback – we're always looking to improve, please could you share with us how you think we can make things a little better?*

Although it's hard to see invective like the hater's above turning into anything useful for you, we have heard stories of quite difficult feedback being transformative for creators. In the early days of their idea, Thom and James from Pizza Pilgrims got into a tangle on Twitter with a rival Italian food business, who accused them of not fully understanding the Napoli-style pizza. Instead of ignoring the feedback, Thom and James got in touch. It was awkward to begin with, but they found out what was behind their comment, and they're now actually collaborators and friends.

Every piece of feedback is an opportunity to learn. Especially the feedback that hurts when you first hear it, this is the stuff we have found the most useful. It pays to take the time to try and understand what was behind it. They may just be unloading on you, but it may just shine a light on something that you can improve.   Thom Elliot

The bottom line is this: someone who cares enough about your idea to give you a point of view on it is potentially one of your most valuable customers. Move towards them, even if it hurts.

Get on the road

I was surprised, as always, by how easy the act of leaving was, and how good it felt. The world was suddenly rich with possibility.
                                        Jack Kerouac, *On the Road*

It's time to start. You don't need much. Just half an idea and a deep breath. Right now you can take the most valuable step in your idea's development – the first one. With nothing but what you have in your hands, you can set off on your Hero's Journey.

Step onto the road and start walking.

· DO IT NOW ·

Here are seven different ways to get started on your idea straight away. Spend five minutes on one or two of these now.

1. Put a meeting in the diary with someone you know who can help you.
2. Book a day off work to start developing your idea.

continued

3. Look online and find someone who has made a similar idea happen, and ask them for advice about how they did it.
4. Call someone you are considering partnering with and invite them to meet to discuss how you're going to make it work.
5. Book tickets to a talk, event or experience that will help you with your idea.
6. Set up a Twitter profile and follow ten people who are in the world of your idea.
7. Set up a Facebook page for your idea.

The first real-life manifestation of your idea – your Version Zero

Ed Foy and Georgie Reames run Press, a juice company. These days they sell their delicious cold-pressed juices out of Selfridges, and their shop in Covent Garden. They launched their product in altogether less salubrious surroundings though . . .

We started by doing a tasting for thirty friends in a pub basement we got for free. We had bought some plastic bottles for a few quid online and £50 worth of fruit. It was the turning point for us – we had a product (a very unpolished one, granted). And we could see everyone's responses, even emotionally and how much they bought into it. Suddenly we were like: 'This is actually an idea! It is a thing! It is no longer a "might". It exists and we can see people are liking it.' We had an idea and it cost £50 to start. We then just incrementally made our experiments bigger . . . we still are. You don't need money to start. You just need the desire.

Ed Foy and Georgie Reames, Press London

What Ed and Georgie did in the pub that day was their Version Zero. Your Version Zero is your first effort. It's your idea in action for the first time. It's you making your idea as cheaply as you can, with just the resources you have available now.

Your Version Zero is a test of your resourcefulness as much as your idea. A good one is *just* enough to bring your idea to life, so that you can experience making it for the first time, and other people can experience using it. Spend as little as you can and have as much fun as possible. Instead of money, use your resourcefulness to get started.

Once you're out in the world with your idea, you are learning. In fact you're in a feedback loop. You try, you learn, you tweak.

Tech companies began this trend. Releasing a 'beta' (trial) version of a website or an app allows a developer to learn from real-life use of their idea, even when it's only half-made. They launch first and tweak later.

What your Version Zero is like will depend on what you're doing, of course. If your idea is to create a sushi restaurant serving only the deadly Fugu fish, you'd better perfect your food prep before you expose customers to it, but the world is getting used to creators doing this now, even in the food industry where Harriot Pleydell-Bouverie of Mallow and Marsh is kicking up a storm:

'I think you have at least six months' grace from customers – where they might think things are a little rough around the edges, but they're OK with it because you've only just started. If you overthink it, and all you do is plan, you don't know what you're planning for. You need to get out with your product and get honest feedback. I was out with these bags of marshmallows – everyone who makes marshmallows bags them. And all people were saying when I was at the market was, "I don't really want to buy a bag because I just want them for myself," or, "I want something a little more gifty than that." So we did our marshmallows in boxes, and I think it's one of the reasons our product has been so popular.'

The thing about making your Version Zero is that you are learning in public. This takes guts. You have to get used to sharing things that are not yet perfect. They are *good enough* for a positive user experience and clear enough to help you learn, but inevitably they will be a little rough around the edges.

In 2006 Tom Mercer was twenty-six and had seen an opportunity in breakfast for busy people like him. One cold Sunday night in February he committed to learning whether it would work.

Shovelling fruit, oats and yoghurt into a series of blenders (he melted four of them as he whizzed his way through the night), he spent all night preparing a hundred samples of his first product – a breakfast shake. He poured it into empty water bottles, stuck a printed label he had designed himself on every single bottle and headed down to Waterloo station at six the following morning to hand out samples to commuters.

'It took me ten hours of working through the night to make 100 products. It was basically just an old Tesco water bottle with a homemade stuck-on label and an oaty, fruity concoction inside. Let's just say that it was just about passable as a product. But that's all it needed to be.'

Cunningly, Tom didn't just give his samples away. He exchanged them for information that would help him improve his recipe and the experience of consuming it. He asked for an email address in return for each bottle, and emailed a short survey later that day for feedback on his shake. Next time he came to the station, his breakfast shake would be even tastier.

'I got the survey results back and on the whole it was really positive and encouraging. People liked the fact it was really filling and that you could have it on the go easily – some people literally drank it walking to work. There were a few people that said that they didn't taste it as they didn't trust the dodgy bloke handing out bottles under the bridge at Waterloo. One girl said that it was really nice but so filling that it made her sick! But it gave me confidence that I was on the right track. I just made sure I made the product even better next time.'

Tom's breakfast shakes were the Version Zero of MOMA Foods. Their bircher muesli and porridge are now stocked by most of the UK's leading supermarkets, and are a feature of a growing number of airline breakfasts. To this day, Tom and his team regularly use this kind of live learning to sharpen their understanding. What could you do like that with your idea? Your Version Zero will of course depend on the type of idea you are planning to build:

1. If it involves food or drink, make it at home. Invite friends and family to sample it and ask for their feedback.

2. If it is hi-tech, make it mid-tech. Mock it up quickly and easily using Prezi or Keynote. Touchscreen laptops are readily accessible these days so you can even make it interactive.

3. If it is an internet business, make an early version of the website. There are many sites that let you do this quickly and often for free (check out WordPress and Drupal, but there are many more in the resources section on theideainyou.com and at the back of this book). Build in a feedback box and then post the link to friends on social media and in relevant chatrooms to get some early impressions.

4. If it is a product, make it as real as you can. Cobble together something that looks or feels like it. Mock up the box the product will come in and share it with friends and strangers to get their initial reactions.

5. If it is an experience, you can try storyboarding it. You can do this using drawings, PowerPoint or new apps like Paper and Storyboard Composer. You could even act it out or make a mood board for it. Anything that lets people experience it and get a sense for how it will feel.

6. If it is a service or business-to-business idea, bring it to life as a sales pitch. Use PowerPoint, or even paper. Write a manifesto for the business. Present it to friends or a friendly 'client'. Approach someone who fits the profile of a future customer. It's amazing how willing to help people will be.

7. If it's an event, put on a slimmed-down version for a group of friends. For instance, if it is a running event, get ten friends and put it on in a local park. If it's a festival – do a one-off show in your garden (maybe ask the neighbours first if this will be OK . . .).

8. If it is a book, design the book cover, and write the blurb for the back. Do a synopsis of each chapter and share it with friends. Write the intro onto a platform like Medium.com and send a link to your friends – see what the world makes of it.

9. If it is a hospitality or leisure business, transform your home into it for a night or weekend. Invite friends to experience it. If your house isn't right then ask around, post on social media or call up venues and ask for a favour. Again, you will be surprised by how willing people are to help.

10. Whatever it is, try making a video describing the concept and how it works. You can see loads of these on Kickstarter. Share it on YouTube. Post a link to it on relevant social media and ask for feedback.

For more inspiration on tools available for making a Version Zero flip forward to the resources section at the end of the book (page 185) and check out the Creator Community at theideainyou.com.

· DO IT NOW ·

Make a Version Zero and put it in front of people to try.

Use only what you need to get your idea off the ground – just enough to start learning. Keep your costs as low as you can and invite feedback from real users.

Find out the following:

- Which users your idea works for and why.
- What you need to learn more about/improve.
- How people are using your idea.

What has surprised you? What was exactly as you expected? If you want to, revert to your concept and update it accordingly.

You are now in a feedback loop. You try something, and learn from it, and then you tweak your product to reflect what you've learned, before putting it out into the world again, to learn again. You are building your idea.

five

DREAMING

I used to think as I looked out on the Hollywood night – there must be thousands of girls sitting alone like me, dreaming of becoming a movie star. But I'm not going to worry about them. I'm dreaming the hardest.

Marilyn Monroe

Imagine a creator.

She lives conservatively, in a small rented house with her husband. She is focused on what she is doing now, making her idea happen, but in her mind she has an image of where she is going.

She loves thinking about the life they will have when their dreams come true. She knows that some people might think she's foolish to do this – that she has 'ideas above her station' – but she's decided to dream anyway, whatever anyone else says. Her dreams get her out of bed every day. They give her energy.

When her idea becomes as popular as she knows it will, they will move out of this small house, and they'll divide their time between Hawaii and Devon. They'll have a nice house in each place. She knows this sounds ridiculous to some people, but it's her dream and it pulls her forward every day. She doesn't just hope it's going to happen; she *knows* it will.

In Devon, she'll pull on her boots after breakfast and explore their land, with her dogs and horses. They'll have a library with a sliding ladder, an open fire and a snooker table. She can already smell the smoke coming from the open fire.

In Hawaii, she can already feel the sun on her back as she walks down the beach.

I want to have the time to think and be in nature. When we get up in the morning, the sun will be coming in through the window. The breeze coming off the sea will bend the trees and create white horses on the water. I'll walk the dogs, and think about what I want to do that day. There'll be a spot in the kitchen where we will have breakfast, with a view of the waves. There'll be music. We'll settle down to work once we've eaten well. There'll be a break for lunch. We'll get in the car with the roof down and head to the café along the beach. Then we'll come back, make calls, create some more art/music/copy and then wrap up with a glass of wine before dinner looking at the sunset. We'll go to bed early and rise with the sun.

You have one life. Step one in ensuring you live it well is exploring where you want it to go and how you would love it to be. This is what we mean by dreaming. In your dream you can have anything. You can live where you please and do whatever you want with your life. It's up to you. In your dream, you assume for a moment that the universe will give you exactly what you hope for, and build a multi-sensory movie in your mind which brings this to life.

Creator story 4: Make what you've always wished for – iEat

Shaz Saleem started iEat, her food company, after more than a decade of craving its existence.

'I'd spent three years at university and my hunger was greatest. Three years away from Mum's cooking having to eat tuna mayo sandwiches and I thought, there must be an opportunity here. The more Muslims I spoke to the more I realized this isn't just my hunger, this is a generation's hunger. This is a generation of Muslims who have grown up in the UK, who feel inherently British, and want to be able to eat the same food their friends eat but can't because they have to eat halal.'

Eventually the frustration built to the point that Shaz realized she had to act:

'It had bothered me for years, then one day I was really hungry and in the

supermarket and I really wanted a lasagne but I couldn't have one. That was the moment I decided to do something about it. I went home and started working on what is now iEat – ethically prepared 100% halal ready meals.'

As far as ideas go, they don't come much tougher to execute than this. iEat is a perishable high-volume product, needing careful preparation and sophisticated supply-chain management. It is also selling into the UK's toughest retail environment. Shaz is made of stern stuff but she was also spurred on by a zeal to satisfy not just her hunger, but the hunger of an entire generation of British Muslims.

· how to do what shaz did ·

Make sure you really care
Before you embark on what could be a journey lasting years, be sure that you care enough to stay the distance. 'I've wanted a shepherd's pie since primary school – it wouldn't go away!' iEat wasn't just a business for Shaz, it was a hunger she just had to satisfy.

Get all the pieces in the jigsaw
Shaz realized that she needed to learn, so she set out to fill the gaps:
'I was only twenty-one – I had no experience – so I got a job at Waitrose. It meant I was able to ask questions. What happens here? Who pays for this space? Who pays for the mark-down on a product when it passes its sell-by date? The next stage was to get a job working for an entrepreneur – I got a job with Peter Jones and worked on Reggae Reggae Sauce, among other things. I learned how you launch big successful businesses and what happens when it goes wrong. In the back of my mind I had iEat as my goal, but I knew I needed to learn first.'

Get help
Shaz doesn't have a background in the food industry. One of the biggest days in the development of her idea was meeting Simon Burdess, a friend of a friend – and former ready-meal buyer for Marks and Spencer. Simon was a significant help in the launching of iEat by helping Shaz understand the food industry, and giving her the confidence she needed to go for it.

Two horizons

In a moment, we'll move on to building a mental image of the future you want to move towards. First, though, we want to make sure there is some balance in this picture.

Imagine two horizons for your idea: one right in front of you and one a long way off in the distance. The one nearer to you is your to-do list, or whatever you use to remind yourself what you need to do today (some people do this from memory). Away in the distance you have the dream – of your idea being fantastically successful.

Creators need both. They complement each other. Just dealing with what's in front of you and doing it day after day will make you forget where you're going. Just dreaming about the future, on the other hand, means you'll never do what it takes to get there. The magic is in having two horizons and striking the right balance between them. You look up from time to time to remind yourself of where you want to go, and then back down to your to-do list, so you can get on and do the things that will take you there.

It's very easy to get bogged down in spreadsheets. The numbers may be important but don't think that it's your business. You have to raise your vision. If you don't have a dream, you don't know where you're going.

Shaz Saleem

Through iEat, her food company, Shaz has solved a problem for a generation of British Muslims by putting halal shepherd's pie and lasagne on supermarket shelves. It's a challenging business and Shaz is one of the busiest women we've ever met. Luckily, as well as a to-do list as long as her arm, she's got a dream which spurs her on:

'Growing up, I didn't have role models who were heads of businesses or successful entrepreneurs. The adults I knew had only moved to the UK in the past ten or fifteen years so they had been working on arriving and sur-viving. My dream is that I might be a role model for people who are in the same place I was ten years ago. I picture myself speaking to a room full of

young Muslim girls like I was, showing them that you don't need to be white, middle class, tall or handsome to be able to be successful in business. It gives me fuel to keep going when times get hard as they do on a journey like this.'

This is how purposeful change happens. Having two horizons for your idea. What you need to do today, and in the distance, glowing brightly, your dream of what you want life to look like in the future.

So, what do you want?

'Imagine you can have anything in your life – what do you want?' It's the ultimate open question.

Have you ever thought about this?

It might feel like a risk to be so expansive. Perhaps you fear that if you go too big in your thinking, and then don't get what you want, you will have failed. Or perhaps you've decided that you're better off aiming low, so you're more likely to get what you want.

Maybe you find it a little unnerving to be asked what you want. It is a hard question! It goes deep – if you have no restrictions, you have to decide exactly how you want things to be.

Perhaps it is culturally wrong for you to think big like this. Perhaps you have people in your life whom you fear would say you should 'pull your neck in' or 'get back in your box' or whatever people say where you live to keep you where you are, to stop you getting where you want to go.

Your subconscious mind is on 24/7. The messages your conscious mind sends it are what it works with. If you want to create a life which is fundamentally different from your current one, you must feed it positive pictures of the future for it to move towards. You have to know what you want.

Design your dream

So – start thinking about your future now. Assuming that things go brilliantly with your idea, what kind of life would you like? Where will you live? What will you do with your time? What will your surroundings look like? What will you do on a Monday morning?

Enjoy thinking about it. Luxuriate in the detail and the feelings that mental future brings you. The more resonant and specific you can make it, the more it will grab you.

Here's how to build a dream:

Collect ideas. As you go about your life, notice what notions attract you. Collect them unedited as thoughts in your mind, or notes in a notebook or even links and images in an app (Pinterest is great for this).

Get vivid. Use all your senses. Use pictures, movie clips, music, sounds, food, fragrance, and sensations in your body. Develop your dream as a multi-sensory presence in your mind and body, by exploring what it looks like, feels like, sounds like, smells like, even tastes like.

Play! Run your future whenever you need it. Access it as medicine when you're down, and a reward when things go well. Keep doing this until the future in your mind glows white hot.

Some steers about building your mental future:

Have fun. This is a creative task. You can have anything you want in this future. Be playful! You are creating an unfettered image of the future to draw you forward. It needs to resonate. If you want flamingos in your garden – they're in!

Don't discount anything. Nothing is ever 'silly', 'unlikely' or in the 'never-going-to-happen' category. This is your future. Resist the impulse to undersell yourself. The whole point is that you can have anything you want.

Make sure it is what you really want. Put flamingos in your dream only if you really want them in your future. If you prefer something a little less flamboyant – maybe a few chickens in a really nice hen house – put that in your dream instead.

Build it together. If you are in a partnership with someone, especially a romantic one, work in tandem. You may have different ways of encoding it in your minds, but having a common dream will make you unstoppable.

Ignore everyone else. They can have their dreams and you can have yours. If you want to live in a small house in the middle of a forest in Sweden, and collect traction engines, then build a detailed picture of that.

Change your dream whenever you want. You don't need to ask permission. What you want from your future will change over time anyway. Anyone who has ever dreamed of being a sports star and then turned forty will know how that works. The only guideline is this: you have to be excited about it.

When you have a dream like this, you have what psychologists call an 'anchor'. An anchor is something with a particularly resonant meaning for you – it inspires significant thoughts which change how you feel. Like the song that reminds you of the good times, or the smell that reminds you of your sweetheart – only this is one you've created deliberately and it's about the future, a perfectly positive future.

You 'fire' your anchor whenever you need it, by thinking about it or looking at it or listening to it. Then it gets to work on your brain, putting you in a good place, reminding you where all this is heading.

Grab a piece of paper and a pen. Get yourself into a playful and hopeful frame of mind. Maybe make a cup of tea – go somewhere you associate with relaxing and feeling good.

First, we want to get a flavour of where you're heading. For now, write down some words and phrases that describe the life you want.

Here's a list to inspire you (but pick your own, obviously!): peaceful, adventurous, stimulating, full of good humour, exploring, home, warm, full of kindness, sunny, cool, interesting, exciting, calm, stylish . . .

Capture between five and ten phrases or words. Then put down your pen.

Now let's switch to thinking visually. Picture in your mind where you want to live in your future.

Where are you?

Think about the topography around the building – are you in the town or country, forest, hills or plains, cliffs or beach?

What does it look like?

Remember – you can have anything you want.

Is your place modern or traditional, large or small? Think about what your house looks like as you approach it on foot. What does the front door look like?

Go in!

What do you see first as you walk in the door? Look around.

Now – where would you like to hang out in this house? Where is most comfortable for you? Go there. Picture yourself there.

Add your family and pets if you like.

Go outside. What do you see when you walk out there? What are the sounds? What's the temperature? Take a moment to soak up the scenery.

Close your eyes and bathe in the detail – make the colours, feelings, the sounds and the scents come alive in your mind. Make them as real and as close as possible.

This is the beginning of your dream. Over time your subconscious will update it – by embellishing it with more detail, or reducing some of the complexity into easy images to access it.

You may want to start playing with a mood board to make this dream more real. Then you can stick it somewhere you'll see it every day, like on the fridge or your mirror, or use it as computer wallpaper. Your dream will come into more focus as you experience things in your life you are drawn to. And then – at some future hour – your dream and your reality will meet. When you get there, we would like it very much if you would invite us around for a ride on those traction engines – or at least please send us a picture.

There is no passion to be found playing small – in settling for a life that is less than the one you are capable of living.

Nelson Mandela

The dream for your idea

When we dream about the future of this book, we imagine seeing someone reading it on a plane. We introduce ourselves and they're pleased to meet us. They tell us it's the best book they've read – they're enjoying it and it has changed how they think about themselves. And thanks to the inspiration and techniques in our book, they are finally creating something they are proud of.

Some people might call this delusional and egotistical. That's nothing. We also imagine seeing it in the *New York Times* bestseller lists and getting a call from someone in Hollywood who wants to buy the movie rights.

This isn't delusional. It's essential. Knowing where you want to get to is fundamental to the success of anything that requires your effort and time. If you focus on the future you want, you can work towards it.

What about you and your idea? If you let your imagination run wild and you think about experiencing outrageous success with your idea – what do you hope will come to pass?

You might see yourself on TV explaining how you made it, or stepping onstage in Stockholm to receive a Nobel Prize, or opening your store on Fifth Avenue, or reading a piece in the newspaper revealing that people in a remote village in Siberia have benefited from your idea, or receiving the keys to your city, or (like us) signing the deal on the movie rights and spilling out into the evening sun in Hollywood for a few celebratory Martinis.

· DO IT NOW ·
the dream for your idea

Look long-term – and dream freely.

Believe that the world will really take to your idea.

What will you see, hear and feel?

When you're starting to experience great success with your idea, what will that look like, sound like, feel like?

Now capture that moment. Turn it up – turn up the volume, the brightness and the colour.

Enjoy looking at it for a while. Get familiar with it. And then, when you're ready, let's get back to that other horizon, the one right in front of you: the work.

six

STAYING FREE

Money won't create success. The freedom to make it will.

Nelson Mandela

In the TV show *The Apprentice*, in which a group of young people compete to impress Alan Sugar into backing their business idea, there is an amazing climax in the closing episodes of every series.

The four semi-final contestants share their vision for their idea. We see them in meetings presenting their plans to a range of experienced business people who ask them hard questions about their ideas and how they intend to turn them into successful businesses. If these meetings go well and they're not 'fired', they get to be one of the two remaining apprentices who develop their idea for a few more days.

The last few days are breathless, as the two finalists pull together a last presentation to Lord Sugar and various other business luminaries, many of whom work in the category they are hoping to transform. They make a TV ad, and develop packaging, a logo and business case and – after a moment to steady their nerves – they step out onto a stage and persuade a live audience (and millions of viewers at home) that their idea is the one to back.

Then Sugar picks a winner – and funds their idea, paying £250,000 of his money for a 50 per cent stake in it.

It makes great TV. There is so much at stake. There is personal transformation, pressure and relief – and what looks like a happy ending: an 'Apprentice' with a bright future under Sir Alan's wing.

But it is a crazy way to begin an idea.

We call this 'weighing the pig before you've caught it'. The Apprentice has to commit to what she believes is going to happen, long before she knows. Before she's worked in the category, often before she's even made a version of her idea, she commits to its future.

Worse, she has to persuade other people that her predictions will come true. She shares her plan of where her idea will go, and tells everyone as confidently as she can that she can take it there, essentially so they will lend her money. And because she's good at painting that picture, and excellent under pressure and has character that Lord Sugar believes in, she gets £250,000 to spend on her idea and a ride in the famous Rolls-Royce.

Once the round of media interviews is over, the real work begins. Those crazy few days racing around London in people movers may have given The Apprentice and her team the chance to iron *some* details out – but it's impossible, even for the most efficient and insightful contestant, to know the future, especially after so little time working on the idea.

Assumptions will have been optimistic. Risks and production details will have been overlooked. With so little time, how could she and her team have understood the complexities involved in delivering her idea? She hasn't started making her idea happen – yet she has committed to its future. And now a major investor has an interest too. She is locked into a vision for her idea that she was forced to formulate for the benefit of the viewing public.

There's more bad news for The Apprentice. Her prediction about how her idea will succeed was almost certainly wrong. Amar Bhidé, a professor at Harvard Business School, did a study exploring how well businesses predict success. Can they pick a winning idea from the start, or do they have to abandon their original plans and find new ways to succeed?

It's an important question if you are in the business of pitching your idea based on a business plan, without knowing your idea well. It's even more important if you're putting quarter of a million quid down on an idea developed in a matter of days.

Of the businesses Professor Bhidé spoke to, 93 per cent revealed that 'the strategy that led to their success was largely different from what they had originally planned'. In other words, more than nine out of ten had changed their business model en route to success. And that was just the successful ones.

So it turns out – though no one's told Lord Sugar – that you'd be seriously unwise to bank on how an idea will succeed from the beginning. In fact, you'd do better if you banked on it changing.

While this is bad news for The Apprentice, it is good news for those who are starting businesses with no outside investment. We *can't* weigh the pig before we've caught it. Having very little money to spend forces us to learn steadily and to create something sustainable, effective and clear over time.

What TV sometimes tells us is that entrepreneurs borrow money against an idea before they've learned how it works. This isn't how it happens for creators, especially those of us who haven't got much money.

What we've found happens for most creators is the following:

You have an idea. It's something you are excited about.

You pluck up the courage to share it with people. You do the cheapest possible version of your idea – just enough to give people an experience of it. Your Version Zero.

You get useful feedback. You start improving your idea – you'll be doing this for its entire life.

You put the new improved version of your idea in front of people. Again and again you do this. You improve it a little each time based on the feedback you get.

You're spending a little money to develop your idea. The minimum. You keep an eagle eye on costs so you stay free enough to explore what your idea can be at its best. You focus on improving steadily rather than growing quickly.

In time your idea creates some energy among the people you have shared it with. You build fans. You're on to something.

Seeing the impact your idea is starting to have, you find new ways to share it and you grow a bigger audience.

In time, you find ways of charging properly for it. Now there is money coming in, which is going some way to covering your costs.

People are talking about your idea. Some people even write about it – so more people hear about it. Fans get in touch with you – giving you ideas, and even what they would pay for them.

Eventually, you reach the point where you are earning more than you are spending. Your idea is becoming a business.

You have now also started some side-projects related to your idea. You're aiming for multiple revenue streams. You want to make the most of the energy in your idea.

Now, with an idea that covers its costs and has a growing number of fans and a range of revenue streams, you have an opportunity to expand more quickly.

You pause. Do you want to borrow money so you can accelerate the growth of your idea? Or do you want to stay free? You weigh up your options.

There are a number of differences between the TV version of idea development and the version most creators experience:

The TV version of an idea is developed in full very early and taken to market as quickly as possible.

The creator version is developed incrementally – starting with a 'light' version – a Version Zero – to see if it works.

The TV version of an idea buys awareness – using paid-for advertising and PR.

The creator version seeks social energy by creating an idea people get excited about, and offering structures to help them share their excitement.

The TV version of an idea depends on the entrepreneur borrowing money early and ceding some control of their idea to an equity partner.

The creator version depends on low-cost exploration of the idea, using free resources where possible – so the creator retains control of the idea until there is clarity about how it works, and often even beyond that point.

The TV version of an idea commits to a business plan.

The creator version commits to starting and learning and may never include a written business plan.

The biggest difference between the two models is the role that money plays:

In the TV version, money is the goal.

In the creator version, money is an enabler of the many small steps the creator wants to take to learn about his idea as he puts it out into the world.

Psychologists love doing experiments about money – and in particular what it does to people. They call money a 'primer' – a behaviour-change trigger. With money as the primer in an experiment, they've shown a falling off in altruism, the collapse of teams and a decline in our receptiveness to others. Money-primed subjects tend to sit further away from each other, are less willing to donate money and prefer solitary activities to collaborative ones. Money, it seems, makes us go weird. You'll know this, of course, from your own experiences. If you have ever lent money to a friend you will know what we're talking about.

The problem with money when it comes to combining it with ideas is that the behaviours that money primes are different from the ones we need to build an idea. When you develop an idea you need to remain open, collaborative and free to explore. Money just doesn't want you to do that.

Without much money available, creators have to learn how to improve their idea in small increments. They work out how it works and how it will create value without anyone breathing down their neck. And because money isn't accelerating things unduly, or creating unhelpful obligations or breakdowns in relationships – creators are able to think clearly and build something sustainable, strong and effective.

Right now, you are free. You don't need to weigh the pig before you've caught it. You are free to nurture your idea from a tiny newborn piglet, one handful of pig-feed at a time, into a prize-winning porker you know well. There will be no difficult conversations with investors, no unseemly haste, no pretending you know what's going to happen before you do, just you improving your idea one day at a time and learning everything you need to know about it.

Start spending proper money on your idea, though, especially other people's money, and you'll step into a different cycle. Your deadlines will tighten and you will lose the freedom to explore and improve your idea at a pace that works for you. It's good to stay free.

Given the destabilizing energy of money, we recommend you define the early years of your idea as an experimental period – when you are starting to learn about what you've got by moving forward *as cheaply as possible*. The early days of your idea are critical because you don't yet know what you have. If you pursue profit too quickly in this phase – before you know how your idea works, how it can earn money, and how to deliver it – you will curtail your freedom. While you still can, stay free, so you can enjoy exploring your idea and create a strong foundation for its future.

How to stay free

These approaches will help you stay free. They will let you remain independent enough to take the time you need to learn about what makes your idea amazing, without commitment or distraction.

Reduce your personal costs

Your own living costs are the real context for the development of your idea. Now is not a good time to buy a new wardrobe or invest in a new car, or a bigger house. Keep your personal costs down so you can stay as free as possible as you develop your idea. Live cheaply, and last longer.

Celebrate small

If something good happens as you develop your idea, celebrate! But do it small. A bloody-minded will to find value in the little things and celebrate with small symbolic gestures will keep money and extravagance in its place. Got your first fan? Celebrate with a packet of chocolate biscuits. Got a sale? Treat yourself to a nice cup of tea. Got a good review? Have extra pepperoni on your pizza tonight. Celebrate modestly and stay free.

Interpret 'investment' in the broadest possible sense

A good night's sleep will pay back the following day. A relaxing and inspiring holiday for you is almost certainly a better investment in your idea than a set of fancy office chairs or a flashy neon logo above the door. Think of everything as a potential investment.

Spend late

When you buy stuff, you raise the stakes. Try to take on costs – especially ongoing costs – at the latest possible moment, and only once you're practically certain they will move the game on.

Wait until you know how your idea makes money before you borrow any

As soon as you have a lender, life gets more complicated. You have someone else to keep happy beyond yourself and your customers. Once you know how your idea will make money, and you can see how you are going to keep doing it, then you can consider an injection of funds to help you expand. By then you'll know what you need and what's superfluous. Until then – and even beyond then, if you can – stay free.

Do things yourself

Doing as much as you can yourself in the early stages of your idea has three major benefits:

- You're cheaper than a professional.
- You'll learn in granular detail how to do what you will eventually ask a professional to do.

- You'll stay closer to the detail of what you're doing, so things are less likely to go wrong.

Harriot Pleydell-Bouverie started Mallow and Marsh, a luxury marshmallow business, in her kitchen. 'Start small and start today is my motto!' she says. She made everything herself, with her own hands, for as long as she could.

'Even when I was getting orders in the hundreds for my marshmallows I was still doing all the labels by hand. It felt too early for me to commission a printer to print thousands and chuck lots of money at it. I know another start-up food business that had to recall hundreds of products as their first batch of mass-produced labels didn't have the right information on them. So, yes, doing it by hand was time-consuming but I was learning at the right pace for me, and I didn't make any expensive mistakes.'

To help you do things yourself, we include a huge range of resources for creators – many of which are free – in Section Four of this book and at theideainyou.com.

Learn how to be resourceful

When creators start out they generally have very little money, and can afford only limited resources. There will be more powerful tools than you have, and higher-quality materials available to those who are ahead of you on the path. You may get resource envy, as you glance over at others in your space.

But what you do have in the early days of refining an idea is an opportunity to explore and hone one of the most critical behaviours in the path of the successful creator – resourcefulness. This is the gift that keeps on giving, even when you are better resourced later in your journey.

When you don't have much, you have to learn how to make it go as far as possible. This is what resourcefulness is. Making more with less. We're trying hard to sweeten a fairly bitter pill here, so we're going to roll out some big guns now. By way of inspiration for your early days as a creator, we offer a short story of the most enduring role models of resourcefulness we know . . .

Astronauts Lovell, Swigert and Haise blasted off in Apollo 13 from the Kennedy Space Center in Florida in the early afternoon of 11 April 1970. They made good headway for two days, but as they neared the moon's orbit, an electrical coil in one of the oxygen tanks caused an explosion, leading to a frightening drop in oxygen and power levels.

It was Jack Swigert's job to fly the Apollo Command Module. He had been brought forward from the back-up crew because the number one pilot was grounded with the risk of measles. It was Swigert who communicated with NASA on the ground, speaking the immortal words, 'Houston, we have a problem' – a cool reaction considering his crew were 200,000 miles from home with oxygen leaking from their space-ship and the temperature dropping fast.

On the ground, Lead Flight Director Gene Kranz ordered the crew to abort their mission. Soon the world was watching the fight for survival as the crews on-board and on the ground in Texas turned their attention to getting Apollo 13 home. They shut down the faulty oxygen tank and the thrusters affected by the explosion. To their horror, they discovered that the carbon dioxide removal system was damaged. They needed this working or the astronauts would slowly asphyxiate inside the module.

Warning lights at Mission Control were showing carbon dioxide hitting dangerous levels. Their only hope of returning to earth was to find a way to fix the damaged CO_2 removal system. The problem was, they didn't have replacement parts aboard.

Mission Control realized they would have to 'jury rig' it – an old nautical term, meaning to make repairs at sea using only what you have to hand.

On the ground, the backroom staff in Houston found an exact copy of the carbon dioxide remover and collected all the parts they knew were on board Apollo to see how they could fix the problem.

What the Hollywood film of the Apollo 13 mission shows so power-fully is that the resourcefulness of the team wasn't so much about resources – it was about their attitude.

In the film, Gene Kranz, controlling the mission from the ground in

Texas, embodies this. Soon after the explosion, while those around him start to lose hope, Kranz, brilliantly played by Ed Harris, steadied the team.

First, he assumed *a positive outcome. He took the decision to believe things would work out, even when they looked their worst:*

NASA Director: 'This could be the worst disaster NASA's ever faced.'

Gene Kranz: 'With all due respect, sir, I believe this is going to be our finest hour.'

Even when he sees other people losing hope, he stays committed. It's a characteristic of resourcefulness – it shows itself in particular when things get tough:

Kranz: 'We've never lost an American in space, we're sure as hell not gonna lose one on my watch! Failure is not an option.'

He – and his team – start to believe that anything *can help them. They look through what their existing resources are meant for, and explore what they* can *do, not what they're meant to do.*

Kranz: 'I don't care about what anything was DESIGNED to do, I care about what it CAN do.'

Like the mighty Gene Kranz, you have what you need. Never let a lack of materials stop you doing what you need to do. Learn how to be resourceful and you will be able to exploit maximum value from every resource – and stay free for longer.

Be on the lookout for new earning models

If you are focused on the different ways your idea can earn money, you will be able to jump on them and use them as soon as they become available.

The world's finest software developers are working for you round the clock. They are developing new ways for your idea to make money, launching new platforms every year which will help you connect your idea with people and their wallets.

These existing free tools will help you stay afloat for longer. They may even become a major source of income for your idea:

- Google AdSense will turn traffic on your website into revenue.
- Affiliate marketing structures (on sites including Amazon, Udemy and thousands of others) will give you a share of any income they earn from customers you send their way.
- Amazon, eBay, Showroom, Greatly and Etsy are global stores for you to sell your products (and even other people's) to an audience of billions.
- society6.com, zazzi.com, redbubble.com and cafepress.com are printing and fulfilment companies which will turn your art-work into T-shirts, posters and even iPhone cases.
- YouTube will sell advertising on your video content and give you 55 per cent of what they earn.
- iTunes will monetize your audio and take a share of the sale.

There are new platforms launching every year which aggregate and connect the many different people and products on the internet – and which will help you make a living from your idea. Start exploring now what's available to help you, and stay connected with the resources information on theideainyou.com which we update regularly.

Creator story 5: Start a movement – Run Dem Crew

'I was running past the Jubilee train yards and there was this huge piece of graffiti on the fence saying, "I want to be in here" – and I just thought, "Yeah, I want to be in here" – I want to be part of this. I don't want to be this person in this body and not able to live in this city. I live in London and it's a very intense city to live in and my body was not of a standard to take the stress of living here so I decided to do something about it.'

Charlie Dark is a DJ, producer and promoter from East London. He started running as a way to get fitter, and soon realized it would help others too. His friends started to see a change in him.

'They noticed I was looking and feeling healthier, so they kept asking can we come running with you?'

Before long he was running regularly with five of his friends.

'We would run a mile and a half every Friday night before we went out. I'd take a picture to prove that we'd done it, post it on Facebook and write a few words. That's how Run Dem Crew really began. We are a collective of creatives and people drawn from across London who run and explore the city under the cover of darkness. In other words we're a running club for people who don't want to run.'

The moment he knew he had to pursue the idea came when Charlie turned up to do his first 5k, a Barnardo's charity run.

'I pulled up in my sports hatchback, no back seats, just a pair of massive speakers, the music going. I get out of the car and I'm wearing my Air Force 1's and basketball top and I'm thinking this is going to be awesome but I look around and I was pretty much the only black guy there. Everyone is really skinny, wearing tiny shorts and looking very serious – and no one was talking to each other. So, I thought, you know what? I need to do some-thing about this.'

And so Run Dem Crew was born.

Run Dem Crew is an alternative to 'stuffy running clubs'. Now, every Tuesday evening, more than 300 people meet to run the streets of Lon-don. They have attracted support from Nike and a huge amount of press. At time of writing – on their thirteenth season – they are at capacity.

In Charlie's mind he wasn't making an idea happen, he was starting a movement. For him, running was a powerful experience – healthy and cathartic – and he wanted to make it accessible to a younger, more urban crowd.

· how to do what charlie did ·

Fill a gap
A movement rises up when there's a hole – where something's not happening that should be happening. Charlie noticed that the amazing benefits of running weren't reaching younger urban people, so he decided to change that.

Focus on getting people to love your idea rather than getting rich

As a creator, it's good to be patient about profit. It's easy to develop a voice in your head that says, 'When am I going to make loads of money?' but it's essential to keep it in its place, especially in the early years of your idea. Business books will tell you that profit (the difference between what you spend and what you earn) is the key to being successful, but we think it's more helpful to focus on building *fans* in the early days of your idea.

I had all of these plans to start big and license Sugru to major chains and it was draining trying to make that happen. It was near Christmas and I felt like I was going mad. I met a friend for a cup of tea and she gave me the best advice I've ever had. Start small. Just try and get two hundred people to love it. Then a thousand. So, that's what we did.

Jane ní Dhulchaointigh, Sugru

Fans create social energy – they post, like and share about your idea – so other people find out about it without you needing to advertise. They save you money. Fans are like a global pressroom with lots of PR staff working for you. The better you are at getting fans and encouraging them to spread the news – the easier it will be to stay free.

In the early days of developing your idea, share it freely so people can experience it and fall in love with it. Give them a positive experience, then help them spread the news about it. Turn them into fans.

We think a good target to aim for is 2,000. With 2,000 fans, you will be starting to create significant social energy around your idea. The economics work at that level too: 2,000 people giving you £20 a year – that's a living; 2,000 people giving you £50 a year and things are starting to get interesting.

That might sound like a lot to you right now, so break it down. Aim for ten. Then a hundred. If you can get a hundred fans, there's no reason you can't get a thousand. If you can get a thousand, you can get two. This is how it works: you and your idea giving people a positive experience and growing one fan at a time.

How much you charge for your idea is one of the biggest levers you can pull. To some degree, how much you ask a customer to pay will depend on the category you're in and how much it costs you to make your idea. There is another principle at work, though, which is worth considering. Charging realistically for your idea might mean you can cover your costs sooner, and that you set the expectation of a high price, but this also puts a barrier between your product and your user so fewer people will choose to experience it. Giving your product away for nothing or selling it at a very low price – if you can afford to – will give the opportunity to experience it to more people.

All the creators we met had found ways of making it easy for people to experience their idea – often removing barriers to purchase completely. They were aware of the importance of getting people to use their idea. They wanted fans.

In the early days, Jane at Sugru gave everyone she met who liked her idea some Sugru for free. She asked them to email her a picture of what they used it for. She kept a wall of them.

'They were like photos from the future, showing me what we could do with the product if we kept making it better and getting more people to fall in love with it.'

This also created social energy around Sugru. People were talking about Jane's idea: liking, commenting and sharing the many stories which her giveaway was stimulating.

Thom and James Elliot from Pizza Pilgrims swapped pizza for opinion in the early days:

'We had just come back from Naples after our trip and we were launching our Berwick Street Market pitch. We were new to the food industry so we just invited lots of bloggers and our followers on Twitter to come and taste our pizzas and tell us which ones we should go with. The response was amazing. We learned a lot about our pizzas but also we found that we built relationships and saw a big spike in social media activity about us. We were overwhelmed, actually.'

Ed Smith and Richard Wilkinson, creators of Doisy & Dam, a fast-growing British chocolate brand which combines chocolate with superfood ingredients, do a weekly 'Chocolate Selfie'. Fans of Doisy & Dam post a picture of themselves consuming it (often with chocolate all over their faces) which show the Doisy & Dam pack. The winner gets free chocolate. Everyone taking part essentially creates free advertising for Doisy & Dam in their Instagram feeds.

Growing your fan base and focusing on giving them a great experience of your idea is the perfect way for you to learn too. When your idea is something you want people to try rather than something you want to make big bucks from, you are able to develop your point of view about how it works with less pressure from customers. It turns your idea into a service for a little while. People will be more likely to forgive you your mistakes, will help you with feedback and will also tend to give you encouragement.

So long as you can cover your costs in this early phase, you will get invaluable experience. You will learn the value of your idea to users and you will learn a lot about the operation of your idea:

- What is the right amount to charge?
- What do you need to consider in terms of supporting the excellent delivery of the product?
- What might you need to invest in as your idea grows?
- What kind of help do you really need?
- What can you do yourself?

Once you have a critical mass of fans and you've taken the learning from that phase, things can change a little. You can turn your thoughts more to making money, and how you might grow even more quickly. You may also want to start thinking about how much you are prepared to share the spoils . . .

Be aware of growth options – and work out what you think of them

We've been very flexible with what happens. Our ambition for the business has grown as the business has grown – it feels quite natural. When we started we were happy to be here – now with a bit of experience under our belt we know more about what we want to do.

Thom Elliot, Pizza Pilgrims

Once there is energy around your idea, and you have clarity about how it makes money, you can pause and work out what you want to do. At this point you have choices. You can take the opportunity to expand more aggressively if you want to. You can roll out more products to more users in more markets. You might want to explore the social impact your idea could have, or build your own personal profile. You might want to look at partnering with adjacent businesses. Or, you can just keep doing what you're doing if you like: enjoying your freedom and making your idea grow. Whatever you do, make sure that you have learned how your idea works, and that you have a fan base of regular users before you do this. You want these developments to be happening from a position of strength. If you do want to expand your idea more aggressively, the conversations you will have with investors, publishers, TV shows and newspapers will be much easier for you if you have the experience of running your idea smoothly and you can show them a growing horde of fans. You will negotiate from a position of strength when 2,000 or 20,000 or 200,000 people are regularly using your idea and loving it.

If you want to, you can seek investment – depending on your ambition and your comfort with sharing the spoils. Unlike the contestant on *The Apprentice*, your vision of the future is likely to be well-grounded now: it will be based on your experience of putting your idea into practice for a few years. Investment – now it's the right time – will help you expand into new markets, develop new variants and improve technology and systems.

It's worth noting, though, that taking on investment implies an end to your complete control of your idea. Most people who would invest in your idea – with the possible exception of friends and family – will be looking to retrieve their money before too long through some kind of exit (venture capital and angel investors normally demand a five-year exit plan). They will want you to seek the sale or flotation of your idea, so that they can take their profit out. In these scenarios, you might end up with a seat on the board, but you'll relinquish some if not most of your control.

A number of the creators we spoke to were keen to stay firmly in control of what they were doing. They took the 'lifestyle' route – just enjoying their idea and earning enough to feel comfortable. No investors, no obligations, and no particularly firm focus on financial growth: just enjoying making something good happen. It is obviously your choice if you want to press the button on growth, to borrow money and share the control of your idea with someone else, but whatever you do, build your knowledge and your fan base first.

Your goal now is to get your first fan.

Share your idea and create ways for people who find it to communicate with you and each other.

Create a Facebook page, a Twitter profile, a Google+ page, an email address.

Somewhere in your idea, make it clear that you would love to hear feedback and encouragement.

Keep sharing your idea and connecting with people who experience it until someone tells you it's awesome. This is your first fan. And once you have fan no. 1 (and you've celebrated with a chocolate biscuit) go and get fan no. 2.

LEARNING

You live and learn. At any rate, you live.

Douglas Adams, *Mostly Harmless*

Imagine a Labrador. Let's call her Bonnie.

There is a man standing in front of her with a bag of treats. He wants Bonnie to learn how to grab a beer from the fridge and give it to him. He's got friends coming round for a poker night.

Bonnie isn't capable of doing this at the moment, so he's breaking it down into steps for her. So far, Bonnie's worked out that she gets a treat for being near the fridge, and another for touching her nose to the rope tied to the door of the fridge. She's doing her best to string the tasks together as the man hoped, but she's not finding it easy.

Bonnie couldn't possibly do this whole trick in one go, so the man is breaking it down into steps. Behavioural psychologists call this *successive approximation*. The man is 'stacking' one achievable step on top of another until such time as Bonnie is able to combine all the moves into one impressive sequence. Even though he's made it as easy as he can for Bonnie, it's still seriously difficult for her. It would be – she's never done this before.

Right now the man is waggling the rope on the fridge door in front of her nose, saying, 'Get me a beer!' The man will reward her as soon as she puts her mouth around the rope, or even gets close, but Bonnie is starting to show signs of frustration: whining, and occasionally even barking. This is testing her. She wants the treats but she is finding it hard to work out how to get them.

Comparing a creator's learning journey to a Labrador's attempts to grab a beer out of the fridge might seem unfair. Learning how to create a chain of restaurants or a bestselling magazine, or a car-sharing website with a million users, or an organic baby-food range – these are complex tasks. But grabbing a beer out of the fridge is too, if you're a Labrador.

Like Bonnie, you will learn one step at a time. Even though your idea might look like one huge seriously challenging whole, it isn't. It is simply a series of steps that you have to learn one after the other. This is how even the most complex tasks become possible. You are building this skyscraper brick by brick.

What's more, as there are for Bonnie, there will be moments when the learning gets hard and when you want to give up. There will be a metaphorical rope hanging in front of your nose and you'll be trying to work out what to do with it. You'll be doing your version of whining and barking because you just can't work it out. What you do next will define whether you succeed.

People usually talk about learning in very positive terms. They talk about the benefits of learning – how it changes your outlook, that it's what life is all about. As human beings we value learning above practically everything else, because it is so transformative.

What most people don't tell you, though, is this: learning hurts. When you are in the process of learning, you go from knowing to *not knowing* in an instant. One minute you know everything – the next you realize that you don't. Not knowing is uncomfortable. This is why people give up. People give up when they don't know how to do something, and they believe they never will.

Making your idea happen is the learning equivalent of masochism. Day after day as you progress, you put yourself in a position of *not knowing*. Over and over again, you face a problem you have never seen before, learn how to solve it, and move on. If you know what to expect from that process – and even better how to enjoy it – you will succeed. In fact, you will be able to do anything.

In this chapter, we're going to show you how to love learning, even the hard bits. We are going to show you how to laugh in the face of things you've never done before. But to show you how to make learning easy, first we need to explain why it can be so hard.

Why learning hurts

In the 1970s a man called Noel Burch came up with an explanation of what happens to us as we learn. His model introduces us to the *hard bit* of learning – the bit when it stops being fun. It's important because it reveals the point when people give up. See if you can see yourself in this:

Imagine you are learning something new. Let's say you want to learn how to drive a powerboat. In fact, let's say you want to get really good at it – you want to learn how to be like the people driving the powerboats in the opening titles of *Miami Vice*. You've found a course you want to do, and you head down to the marina.

Noel Burch's model shares the four stages you can expect to pass through as you move from enthusiastic novice to stunt driver (via some slightly less attractive states). Let's go through them now:

Stage 1: Unconscious incompetence (the ignorance is bliss phase)

You look at the boat you're going to learn to drive and you think, 'It can't be that hard, can it? Surely you just jump in, turn the key, push that lever forward – and you're off?'

At this point, you don't know how little you know. You have no idea what is involved in handling a 300 horsepower RIB. Because it looks easy, you add assume it is. Ignorance is bliss. For now.

What someone who is about to build an idea might say in Stage 1: 'I can't wait to get started on my idea – it's going to be a blast! I'm going to be RICH!'

What to do while you are in unconscious incompetence: Unconscious incompetence feels good. It is useful because it creates the energy to learn. Use your naive enthusiasm to get started! But beware: a much less enjoyable stage is lurking just round the corner . . .

Stage 2: Conscious incompetence (the really hard bit)

Back at the marina, you're in the briefing room preparing for your first drive in the powerboat. You've been here all morning. The instructor is briefing you to prepare a waypoint plan for your crossing today, with reference to safety, the tides, navigation and weather. You've been given a three-inch-thick reference book with local tides, depths and waypoints, and the latest weather forecast. You still haven't got in the boat.

Inevitably, the moment has arrived when it's dawning on you that there is more to driving that boat than you thought. Welcome to the hard bit, which happens whenever anyone learns anything: the moment when you realize how little you know.

How to recognize when you're in conscious incompetence: People usually get annoyed at this point. When learners hit conscious incompetence and realize how little they know, they often try to denigrate the skill they're trying to learn, or even the person teaching it to them. They hunt for ways to justify stopping – so they don't have to endure the discomfort of not knowing any longer and they don't have to feel bad about giving up.

What you might say when you hit conscious incompetence while you're making your idea happen: 'I'm obviously not cut out for this. You have to be more of an "entrepreneur" than I am. I'm way too nice for this. I'm going to stop kidding myself that I can do this and go back to working for someone else.'

What to do when it happens to you: Laugh at yourself for being so predictable. Notice how it feels not to know everything for once. And push on. The only way out is through. Get used to this feeling – you're making something happen that no one has ever done before – from scratch. This isn't getting a beer out of the fridge. This is your life's work.

Stage 3: Conscious competence (concentration still required)

Back on your powerboat course: Well done. You stuck with it and you're through the hard bit. With a bit of application, your learning is starting to pay off. Learning about tides and weather systems looked really hard, but was easier than you thought, and also vital for safety. You're glad you pushed on. And the fun of driving around in that boat has begun.

You're still some way from mastery – it takes real concentration for you to control the boat – but you can feel your skills growing. You make the odd mistake, like crashing into a buoy and almost running aground, but you decide not to be embarrassed about them – you are developing a new capability, after all, so it's not surprising that you make mistakes. And you know that focus and concentration will lead you to mastery in the end.

How to recognize when you're in conscious competence: People pull funny faces in this stage, because they have to concentrate so hard. You see people sticking their tongue out in concentration, and pulling effort faces. This phase is also tiring because of the attention required to do the task you're learning, so you can expect to feel pretty exhausted afterwards.

What to do: Keep practising – mastery awaits.

Stage 4: Unconscious competence (mastery)

Unconscious competence is mastery. You've been through the hard bit of learning and spent enough time practising to be able to do the task well. Now you can do it so well, in fact, you don't even need to think about it. You are unconsciously competent.

You won't reach unconscious competence on a training course. The key to reaching this stage is practice. If you really want to feature in the opening titles of a *Miami Vice* remake, you can expect to have to spend years in your powerboat learning how to handle it safely so you can look that cool. No effort faces are allowed in opening titles.

How to recognize when you're in unconscious competence: Most people know unconscious competence the best from driving. If you have been driving a while, you've probably had the experience when you realize you have been driving for several minutes and you have practically no recollection what happened. You were so lost in your thoughts that you ate up the miles while they were outside your awareness. This is unconscious competence. You're so competent at driving, sometimes you even find yourself doing it without thinking about it. Compare that to when you started driving!

Having the space to think about other things is the hallmark of unconscious competence. It's why great footballers have 'time on the ball' – they don't need to think about dribbling the ball or keeping possession, they have the space to focus on where the other players are and how to build a great move. It's why expert musicians can explore their performance of a piece too – as they've already got the notes nailed and the dexterity to play them, they can get into what they're trying to say.

In summary, here is what Burch is saying learning feels like, from start to finish:

- This is brilliant – I love new things!
- Yikes! This is harder than I thought!
- This is terrible!
- I am terrible!
- Actually, I might be OK . . .
- Yes! This *is* amazing. I am amazing!
- Now, what was it I needed to buy at the supermarket later . . . ?
- [OK, we made that last one up.]

As you learn how to crack the many new tasks you take on, you will inevitably hit conscious incompetence (the hard bit) many times. It is as inevitable as autumn following summer. You just can't skip it.

What you can do, though, is notice it. It can actually be funny, seeing how you react to hitting the hard bit. You might find yourself saying, 'This is a total waste of time!' or turning on yourself and moaning, 'I'll never get my idea off the ground!' You might even feel like throwing your phone or computer out the window. However you react, the solution is the same for everyone: keep going. It's always about to get better.

As you create your idea, you will be doing something new every day. This is why it's such an amazing experience – but it's also why people give up. Learning is painful sometimes – especially when we realize how little we know. How you respond to this is crucial to your success. It's probably the biggest deciding factor in your success as a creator – your ability to respond to the *hard bit* in learning. If you roll over, deciding that it is too hard and that you won't ever be able to do it, you will not succeed. If you notice what's going on, and choose to laugh at yourself and push on, you will – and gloriously.

Never assume that because you don't understand something that you can't understand it. Everything can be learned. Have faith in your ability! Continually remind yourself that when you try something new you won't necessarily fail.

James Kennedy, Kennedy City Bicycles

Amen. Everything can be learned.

Creator story 6: Solve a local problem – parkrun

Back in 2004 Paul Sinton-Hewitt had picked up an injury, and was kicking his heels at home in south London. As a keen club runner, he was surprised that there weren't any free, easy-access running events in London. People would want that, wouldn't they? He knew he would when he was back on his feet.

With a bit of time on his hands he decided to test his hunch and set one up himself. Out of the back of his car, he put on a free 5k run at 9 a.m. on Saturday, 2 October 2004 in Bushy Park, London. Thirteen runners turned up – a mix of friends and local runners.

The feedback was good, so Paul decided to do another one the following week – same time, same place.

Over the next twelve months, Paul kept the run going and the numbers grew as word of mouth spread. During that time Paul improved the idea, and gave it a name: 'UK Time Trials'. Using his coding skills, he built a simple online registration and result-processing system.

After eighteen months of hosting a run every weekend, Paul realized that the numbers in Bushy Park had grown so large that he would have to open a new run in another park nearby. Duncan, one of the runners at Bushy Park, agreed to set up and manage the new run under the UK TT brand. Over the next two years, ten more runs sprang up.

Paul kept polishing his idea and operating systems, and decided to change the name to parkrun to better reflect the spirit and promise of the brand.

Eleven years later, parkrun has more than 300 weekly events in eleven countries, with over 100,000 runners. That's more than three London marathons – running every Saturday morning at 9 a.m. And here is the killer stat: 0% churn. Every parkrun which has been launched has continued.

With over a million registered members, parkrun is on course to be the world's largest grass-roots sports organization. The biggest brands in sport have come knocking – and some are funding its expansion. Paul also has a CBE propped up on his mantelpiece.

· how you can find an idea like paul did ·

Take time out if you can
Paul was unlucky to get injured, but he took the chance of the time and unused energy his hiatus gave him to make new connections and allow ideas to take place. Time out will help you to look at things through fresh eyes, and find the energy to give ideas a go.

Use what you have
Notice what you are good at, and in time the connections will begin to form and crystallize into an idea – just as they did for Paul.

'I knew I was a technologist, I knew I could manage change and I knew I could get people to do things. I needed to find something that had those three elements in it.'

Develop an ethos

Paul knew what he was trying to do with parkrun – he wanted it to be available as a free run for as many people as possible.

'I'm not that ambitious about worldly goods so I can protect this model. parkrun is a social enterprise – it's for people and their community. We keep it simple, and focus on the things we do well – we don't get pushed into areas of exploration that weaken what we do.'

Commit to your community

Building a community like this needs commitment from you. People need to know you are going to be there.

'I was committed to make it carry on for ever, but I had no idea how I would fulfil that commitment. You just have to have faith you will. I have managed to find help whenever I needed it.'

Find the engine in your idea

Paul realized early on that the timing data was valuable, because it would give runners a reason to stay interested – and to keep coming back and improving their times.

'I realized that that data I was collecting would allow me to build more and more interesting facts about the runners, so I started an Excel spreadsheet and it evolved into an amazing database.'

Never ever give up

From the very first run, Paul captured the runners' times, wrote a report and sent it to the local newspaper. And kept doing it until they printed it.

'I knew they would become interested if I wrote interesting copy and I included a photograph. They ignored me so I did it the next week and the next week and I carried on doing it. Eventually they started to publish it.'

Find out more about Paul's story at theideainyou.com.

Introducing the mindset for learning

Everything can be learned, but how do we access that faith – that belief in our ability to succeed? It's down to your mindset. Professor of Psychology at Stanford Carol Dweck has shown there are two key mindsets people have when learning. One leads to learning breakthroughs and the other leads to people throwing their toys out of the pram when things get a little challenging. With the awareness of these, and especially of your own default learning mindset, you will be able to learn anything you need to.

First there is what she calls a 'fixed mindset'. People with a fixed mindset believe that their capability is static. They say things like 'you've either got it or you haven't'. To someone with a fixed mindset, you're either artistic, sporty, good at public speaking, good at driving, good with animals, or you're not. You're either good at being a creator or you're not.

Professor Dweck has shown that, above all, people with a 'fixed mindset' want to appear capable. They try to avoid appearing incompetent at all costs – usually because of their early educational experiences. Their teachers and parents generally only said 'Well done!' when they got an excellent result in a test, rather than when they simply tried hard.

For them, being not very good at something is a sign they really shouldn't be doing it. They believe incompetence is shameful. They hate not knowing what they're doing – so they walk away when they feel too challenged, muttering about how much of a waste of time it is.

Ever had a fixed mindset? Hmmm. Us too.

You will not be able to develop your idea into something amazing if you have a predominately fixed mindset. You will encounter so many tasks you've never done before, and you will be consciously incompetent at most of them at first. With a 'fixed mindset', you will want to give up just when things are getting interesting – just when you should be pushing through the agony of not knowing to the point where you do.

What people with a fixed mindset don't realize is that everyone is a little sketchy the first few times they try something. It's part of learning. It doesn't mean you're incapable. It just means you're a novice.

The great news is that changing your mindset is much easier than learning how to be good at everything.

To succeed in this Hero's Journey, you must cultivate what Professor Dweck calls a 'growth mindset'. With a growth mindset, you expect to find new tasks hard – and you do them anyway. With a growth mindset, you are not fixated on whether you will succeed or fail; you are focused on what you will learn. You view the temporary pain of not knowing as a signal to push forward rather than an excuse to give up and say how annoying everything is. You know you need to persist in order to learn.

The difference between these two mindsets is between someone who wants to look smart and someone who is comfortable looking a little less than competent while they learn. Which one are you?

Expect wisdom not resolution

As the circle of light increases, so does the circumference of darkness.
Albert Einstein

The nature of complex tasks is that the learning never really ends. Just as soon as you've learned how to do one thing, another you don't fully understand appears. You are moving the game on constantly, but every time you do, you reveal how much more there is to learn.

This cycle of learning is never-ending but there is some reassuring news. Although you will never know everything, you will become progressively more comfortable with not knowing. Learning to deal with this paradox – that resolution never really comes despite your relentless problem solving – is probably one of the deepest personal lessons offered by the process of developing an idea.

Hunching – how to keep going when you don't know the answer

As you go on the journey of making your idea happen, you will find that you spend much of your time not knowing exactly what to do.

To operate comfortably in this situation, you have to do some 'hunching'. Hunching is what you do when you don't yet have the answer. Giving your best guess. Hunching is making it up as you go along because you need to keep going even though you aren't sure. It's what everyone's doing. We are all making it up as we go along.

In terms of answers, hunches are pretty much all you will have for much of the life of your idea. You can't possibly know everything – no one does – so you decide to hunch about it.

Here is an example of hunching in action:

'I don't know for sure, but my hunch is that people will be more excited about this if we make it in bright colours. I see lots of brightly coloured fashions on the high street these days.'

Note – this doesn't mean that it would be wrong to do it in dark colours, or that it will definitely work in bright colours. It just means that this person has a feeling that bright colours will work, and they've been smart enough to share their hunch.

Here's another:

'I have a hunch – and it's just a hunch at this stage – that we're going to need to give people the chance to try out the location-based reminder to demonstrate how well it works.'

Note – this person is communicating brilliantly. She is wise enough to let the person she is talking to know that she is not certain about her view, that this is just a hunch at this stage, but she still wants to share her idea so they can discuss it.

Who knows what could happen as a result of this conversation? The team might decide to develop a free demo of the location-based reminder in action so that they can play it on You-Tube. Feedback on the video may help them learn how useful it is. They may even find that sales rise when people view the video. All this experimentation comes from our clever friend being brave enough to share her hunch. She wasn't certain (people rarely are), but she thought she'd share her hunch anyway.

As you progress your idea, you will have to make things happen based on your hunches – because you will rarely know exactly what to do. The great thing about hunching is that it sets you free from being 'right'. There is no absolute truth anyway. Making your idea happen is essentially a series of experiments. You don't know what the right answer is so you try on a few possibilities and see which fits.

There is a scene in the film *The Social Network* where Mark Zuckerberg, the founder of Facebook, is arguing with Eduardo Saverin, one of his early partners, about whether they should be running advertising on the site to raise capital and start to turn a profit.

Saverin: 'It's time to monetize the site . . . we have 4,000 members.'
Zuckerberg: '. . . How do you want to do it?'
Saverin: 'Advertising.'
Zuckerberg: '. . . The Facebook is cool. If we start installing pop-ups for Mountain Dew it's not gonna be . . . We don't even know what it is yet. We don't know what it is, we don't know what it can be, we don't know what it will be. We know that it's cool, that is a priceless asset . . .'

This is hunching in action. The founders of Facebook didn't yet fully understand what their idea was, but at that point Zuckerberg had a strong hunch that providing people with a clutter-free platform from which to communicate and express themselves was a priority over driving advertising revenue. He wasn't saying that they should never run advertising on the site – look at Facebook now! – he was just using his hunches to inform and guide the development of his product at that point.

A pocket guide to hunching:

At the start, see your idea as just a series of hunches. It will set you free from having to 'crack it', and give you permission to explore.

You can have multiple hunches running at the same time. Hunches about who will buy your idea, why they might need it, how it should be made, where you should sell it – the list is endless.

Contradictory hunches can co-exist too. Hunching allows you to explore different points of view. You don't need to be right.

If you're working with other people, it's good to create an atmosphere in which hunching is welcomed. If you work in a team, get everyone using the term 'hunch' – it means fewer arguments, and more momentum.

Hunching is essentially about letting go of being 'right' – there are going to be so many things you don't know in the life of your idea that you will rarely if ever be 100 per cent right about anything, so why not hunch!

In the world of making new things happen, we are all making it up as we go along. Getting comfortable with this process is the basis for making your idea succeed. If you can enjoy the experience of learning as you develop your idea, you will enjoy the journey.

· DO IT NOW ·
start practising hunching

Grab a pen and paper and do some hunching about the following questions. Use a pen and paper, because then you'll do the work. **DO IT NOW**!

Write down your hunches about the following:

- What are you going to enjoy most about making your idea happen?
- What are you going to find most challenging?
- What is the key to success for your idea?

The Future for Your Idea

eight
WORKING OUT YOUR IDEA'S *WHY*

If you don't stand for something you'll fall for anything.

Malcolm X

Beyond earning some money and giving you something to do with your time, what is the point of your idea? Looking outside what you hope your idea will do for you – and towards what you hope it will do for the world – *why* are you doing it? What change is it going to create? Why is it important that it exists?

We call this your idea's *why*.

A *why* is probably the most powerful branding idea around – because people buy into *why* you are doing something as much as *what* you are doing. Having a clear *why* means you can write a story in your customers' minds about why your idea exists – and why it matters. It gives people a reason to support you. It turns your idea into an ideology.

With a *why*, a florist can transform his shop into a place for helping people show their love for each other, or into a celebration of all that is beautiful and natural in the pastures and meadows of this country. If he has a *why*, he's doing more than just selling flowers: he's changing the world.

Having a *why* switches a model railway blog from being just a showcase of OO-gauge model railways and craft ideas, into inspiration for your inner engineer, or a place to lose yourself in the miniature world of your imagination.

A jeweller with a *why* buys gems and other precious materials just like any other – but she sees her business as a way of creating family treasure. Her *why* changes the conversation with her customers too. A necklace becomes more than just a set of interlinking gold chain loops with a pendant; it's an heirloom. Her atelier is more than a display of jewellery; it's a cache of wonder, and the jumping-off point for family histories. Her *why* puts meaning into what she creates. Her *why* makes the valuable priceless.

Our favourite ever version of a *why* is from an ad by Apple Computers in 1997:

> Here's to the crazy ones. The misfits. The rebels. The trouble-makers. The round pegs in the square holes. The ones who see things differently. They're not fond of rules. And they have no respect for the status quo. You can quote them, disagree with them, glorify or vilify them. But the only thing you can't do is ignore them. Because they change things. They push the human race forward. And while some may see them as the crazy ones, we see genius. Because the people who are crazy enough to think they can change the world, are the ones who do.

Apple's *why* was to support a group of people, 'the crazy ones': people like Einstein, Picasso, Jim Henson, Gandhi, who featured in the photos which accompanied that campaign.

When we see that campaign, we think – 'YES! The crazy ones are important! We need more people like that in the world! We identify with them. We want to be part of the movement.'

These days it's more important than ever to have a *why*. Most creators don't have the money to spend on advertising and PR. Small businesses tend to have to build awareness through word of mouth. A good *why* is rocket fuel for your idea's story. It's what your customers will tell their friends when they talk about your idea. It will provoke likes, comments and shares. It will inspire them to say: 'Look at what I've discovered! I like these guys. I agree with what they're trying to do.'

The best kind of *why* not only has meaning for your customers, it also has meaning for you. We have a *why* for this book – which matters to us, and has kept us going through the hard work of writing it. This is from our notes when we were preparing our publisher proposal:

> We believe that everyone has an amazing idea inside them, one that will change their life and maybe even the lives of many others. But we are led to believe that we need to be special to make our ideas happen by the way entrepreneurs are portrayed on the TV. We are here to tell people that you don't need to have an attitude, an MBA, or lots of money to make their idea happen. You just need to care about your idea, be armed with a few simple tools and techniques – and be prepared to put one foot in front of the other through thick and thin. Our book will help normal people change their lives by helping them to make the amazing idea in them happen.

For us, helping people realize their ideas is a more inspiring purpose than 'to become a published author' or 'to show a book with my name on the front to my mates'. With this purpose in mind, we know why our book really matters to us, so we keep going in any case. There's a good feeling for us as we write it.

Our *why* has also helped us decide content. If we thought something would help people succeed we would include it. We knew we should write about getting your head straight because we want a wide range of people to find the book valuable – not just those who have done this sort of thing before. We knew that we had to write about looking inside to find something you really care about, because many readers won't be motivated by money alone.

It also helped us understand what to leave out. All we needed to do was to ask, 'Will this help people make their ideas happen?' If the answer was 'no', we hit delete – especially if we realized we were only including that content to look clever.

A great *why* will inspire great stories

Sugru has a very clear *why* which plays a central role in its marketing. Jane ní Dhulchaointigh – its inventor – is very clear that Sugru is more than just a material to fix and improve things around the house. It's a way of empowering people to take charge and make their stuff work better for them.

'We throw too much away. Products are so cheap these days that we don't even learn how to fix them or to make small modifications to improve them, so things end up in landfill. Sugru is a material that will make the things in our lives last longer and work better.'

Sugru's *why* is clear in the language used on its packs, its website and across its social channels: 'Invented to make fixing and making easy and fun'. The website is built around thousands of examples sent in by fans using Sugru to make small improvements inside and outside the home. Small improvements that often make a huge difference to people's lives. This growing community is a source of stories showing people outside the community *why* they need Sugru. It's the perfect marketing idea: it engages the product's customers, it creates content people want to share, and it showcases what the product can do.

What story can you create in your customers' minds about the change you are trying to create in the world with your idea? What would a community of people who love your *why* be doing?

Creator story 7: Turn pro with your hobby – Decorator's Notebook

In 2011, Bethan John started her design blog, Decorator's Notebook, as a hobby. She was simply loving writing about the interiors products she found and enjoyed showing them on her site. Bethan's interest was small independent designers. In particular she focused on the low-volume artisanal designers that were rarely featured in the magazines she wrote for, because they made their products in such small numbers and couldn't meet the demand created by the major magazines.

'It never occurred to me that anyone would read what I was doing. I thought the stuff was beautiful and I enjoyed it. But people started reading the blog and over time the numbers grew and I got better at writing about subjects my readers enjoyed. Then people started telling me, "It would be cool to have somewhere to buy these beautiful things!"'

Bethan saw the opportunity, and it felt right to her, to help these small-scale designers connect with people who wanted to buy their products. She decided to make Decorator's Notebook her sole focus.

She quit her magazine job and teamed up with her brother Joe: 'It all made sense – I am not competent with web design or finance – and he was working in e-commerce for a university so there was a great fit.'

They revamped the website so it could sell products. Now they source and sell independent, ethical products to customers all over the world.

· how to do what bethan did ·

Give before you get
Bethan wrote her blog consistently for years, without monetizing it. She loved doing it and built a widespread reputation for high-quality content. By the time she launched her business, she had credibility with her readers.

Stay open to opportunity
Decorator's Notebook became a business because Bethan responded to what her fans were asking for. She had a dialogue with them which helped her understand what they wanted, and she changed her business accordingly.

Become an authority
Decorator's Notebook specializes in ethical products, and has an eye out constantly for innovation in the world of such products – even if they don't fit the brief for the shop. They have a passion for a particular zone in the design category – and enjoy learning more every day.

Know your enemy

Knowing your *why* isn't only about knowing what you're for. It is also useful to know what you're against. It gives you something to fight, something to improve on. As we saw in chapter 4, Tom Mercer's MOMA Foods makes fresh breakfast smoothies, porridge and bircher mueslis. But they don't just make breakfast products. They're against something too. They're on a mission to eliminate bad eating habits. There are a lot of early starts in the breakfast business, and this is the *why* that gets them out of bed every morning:

We will revolutionize breakfast by banishing bad breakfast habits and providing the best breakfast on the market.

MOMA Foods wall poster

Who or what is in the way of the change you want to see? Do you know your enemy? Do you have a sense of fight in you? What do you want to fight against? Who will support you in your fight?

Your dilemmas help you work out your *why*

Mark Parker, CEO of Nike, tells a story about meeting Alexander McQueen. The fashion designer had been in touch with Nike. He wanted to design a range of exclusive co-branded McQueen/Nike trainers. Mark took his time over his response, and consulted people back at Nike's Portland HQ. It was an interesting offer: one of the world's leading designers was hoping to create some shoes. They could sell in the hundreds of thousands if not millions.

But Mark knew it wasn't the right thing to do.

Nike is a sports performance brand, not a fashion brand. Everything it does is designed to help athletes perform better. At Nike, performance always comes first – before fashion or even aesthetics. This is how Nike builds and retains their performance pedigree. And this is why Mark Parker said no to Alexander McQueen. The dilemma he faced hardened his resolve on this.

Over time, your idea will also face dilemmas – in particular about what you do and don't do. How you face these dilemmas will sharpen your conviction around your *why*. It certainly worked this way for Bethan John:

'I think in the first year of business . . . the main journey has been us working out what Decorator's Notebook is. We have had to work out what we do and what we don't do. If anything's vague in your head, you can bet it's ten times as vague in your customer's head. Now we are much sharper at looking at something and knowing what we should do. We are much clearer about what Decorator's Notebook is and isn't.'

As its popularity increased, Decorator's Notebook was approached increasingly often with requests to feature 'sponsored posts'. Essentially these were offers of money to write about products sold by other retailers. This was a dilemma for Bethan and Joe.

'We realized that, for us, it's about becoming an authority – so it had to be about ethical design in a wide sense. Every product we sell will have a social story behind it – and we won't sell our space to people who don't. Some of the talent around the world is incredible. Decorator's Notebook is a showcase for those people.'

Bethan and Joe's *why* became clearer when they were confronted with a dilemma. They had to resolve an issue they weren't comfortable with to remind themselves what they care about.

Faisel Rahman runs Fair Finance. His company is a social business which makes loans to people the banks won't lend to, so that they can get their lives back on track. His *why* is clear to him – to put loan sharks out of business – but the detail of his ideology was tested early on.

Three weeks into the life of his idea, he had to decide whether to take his first defaulting client to court.

'I was thinking – do I really want to take this woman that I know to court? I actually know her. I know the names of her kids. But neither of her two

friends that vouched for her are now willing to back her. We had exhausted absolutely every option in trying to contact her and resolve the situation. I knew it would mark her credit file for the next six years. She may even be declared bankrupt. Am I then not just pushing her back into the hands of loan sharks? I knew it was an important question.

'In the end it came down to this: If I don't enforce and honour the contract of trust that we have entered, how can I honestly walk into a meeting with anyone and say that Fair Finance is building a relationship based on trust and responsibility on both sides? It has to work both ways. So, in the end – and I didn't like doing it – I took her to court. It was the right thing to do – we have put trust at the heart of our lending, so if it's broken there has to be a cost.'

Faisel tells this story because it explains a lot about Fair Finance's philosophy. It's also Faisel's favourite interview question – to ask people what they would do in that situation. It shows him how that person thinks, and helps him understand whether they have the moral perspective that will work at Fair Finance.

'I'm not looking for a straight yes or no, I'm looking to see if they would do everything they can to help the person and stop that happening first, as that's the ethos of this business. That lending money is about people not procedure.'

It's in these momentary dilemmas that you learn more about your idea's *why*. Over time you build the story of your idea and why it has to exist.

A good *why* inspires folklore

A *why* will create stories around your idea. The decisions you make over the years will be handed down to other people connected to your idea as powerful reminders of what you stand for. These help you build your culture and they give you something to draw on when you need to make tough calls in the future.

The Alexander McQueen story is handed down through Nike to bring to life their ideology about performance as their priority. It really has become Nike folklore. The story explains to people who work at Nike what they will and won't do – and why. The past is helping people make decisions in the future.

Paul Sinton-Hewitt started parkrun back in 2004. Eleven years later parkrun has over a million registered members and 100,000 people take part in a parkrun every week. His *why* was to provide a service in the community – a 5k run on a Saturday morning at 9 a.m. He wanted people to be able to connect with each other and for them to get the health benefits of running. Paul made a promise to himself early on that parkrun would be free to enter – forever. It was central to his idea that running is good for community. In his view, it shouldn't cost anything to run in your local park. This is the world he wanted to create and protect.

His promise has been tested many times as big global brands have come to him with money and a slightly different vision for what parkrun could be.

In the early days of parkrun Paul Sinton-Hewitt turned down an offer in the hundreds of thousands from a big UK sports organization, principally because it required parkrun to charge runners a fee to take part. He said no, and parkrun is still free. It wouldn't be parkrun if it wasn't.

'If this was started by the will to make money then I would have jumped at those offers. But I took the view very early on that parkrun was for the community. It is about people and their lives. Our focus is on growing communities, not revenue. It makes it easy for us to protect the idea too – if anything makes it harder for people to run or if anything is not in the community's interest, we just won't do it.'

Over time, stories will accumulate around your idea. This is its folklore – showing you and the world what you and your idea believe in. Like Nike, Decorator's Notebook, Fair Finance and parkrun, you can expect your principles to be tested, even early in the life of your idea – so it's wise to have a point of view about *why* it exists, beyond simply being something that you want to get bigger.

Why does your idea need to exist? Beyond your own life, what will it change as it succeeds? What is the story that you are giving people to follow?

Of course, your idea's purpose will become clear over time, as you are faced with dilemmas you have to respond to, but for now have a go at writing an early version of your *why.*

Some criteria to help you develop a great *why* for your idea:

- It's a change to the world that you care about.
- Your customers will also care about it.
- Your idea can credibly deliver against it.
- It inspires ideas and helps you know what you will and won't do.

Do it in the space below or on a scrap of paper. It may be helpful to you to hand-write your *why* as it will feel like it comes from your own body. This will make it easier to hold in your mind as you shape your idea.

Our reason for being is:

. . . .

. . . .

. . . .

. . . .

As an extension to this exercise, why not create a piece of art based on your *why* – something which will continue to inspire you. Sarah Corbett at the Craftivist Collective, a movement that helps people voice their opinions through creativity and craft, has a message on the inside of her craft suitcase which inspires her every time she opens it.

Never doubt that a small group of thoughtful, committed citizens can change the world; indeed, it's the only thing that ever has.

Margaret Mead

She has – of course – stitched it herself.

nine

BE YOURSELF

If you end up with a boring miserable life because you listened to your mom, your dad, your teacher, your priest, or some guy on television telling you how to do your shit, then you deserve it.

Frank Zappa

Copying how someone else has done something is one of the most effective ways to solve problems. Psychologists call it 'modelling' – and it is nothing to be ashamed of. Life is much too short to do all our own learning so why not learn from other people's experience? It's why we have teachers. It's why we seek advice.

Want to know how to be a good parent? Ask someone with lovely kids. Want to know how to hold a room's attention? Watch a stand-up comic, an after-dinner speaker or a politician. They've done the learning – and you can benefit from it. It's copying without cheating.

Modelling shortens the learning curve for all of us. Finding out how someone else solved your problem is often the best place to start. It's what a good proportion of the internet is dedicated to: people who have knowledge and expertise sharing it so we don't have to work everything out for ourselves.

This book is one big exercise in modelling. We are sharing what we have learned, and including a wide range of creator stories, precisely so you don't have to do the years of learning they and we did. You can model it instead.

But modelling will only get you so far. If all you do is copy how other people have done things before you, you will create something operationally sound but empty of originality. You will create an idea that is effectively disembodied. It's an idea, but it's not really yours. You are missing out on the most magnificent of opportunities in the noble journey of bringing your idea into the world. You are missing out on your opportunity to *let your light shine* – and this is where the fun lives.

When you start an idea, you create a new territory in which you have *agency*. Here you have the freedom to create outcomes that you care about. You have shown the courage to set out on your own. Now – if you have the courage to be yourself – you can create something utterly original. Why not change the world in a way that you believe in? Don't do it how *they* do it – do it how *you* do it!

During your journey, you will often find yourself wondering what you should do in a certain situation. As different challenges crop up, you may be tempted to switch to modelling mode. Who else has faced this? What did they do?

Technique is easy to model. Tone of voice, style and approach aren't. By all means emulate other people in the approach they take to solve problems – but make sure you are asserting your own style and beliefs too.

Being yourself is good for your health. You use less energy than when you're pretending to be someone else. You have more fun too. You're being what psychologists call 'congruent'. There is no hiding going on, no pretending, no disconnection between what you think, feel and believe and how you are living. Just you being yourself – and being happy that way.

If you think there is something a little imperfect about you, you are right. Like every human being, you are fallible, variable and different from everyone else. But what if this is your secret weapon? What if you are exactly who you need to be to make your idea fantastically successful? What if you are exactly the right person to create an idea that is original, authentic and world-changing? What if it is actually *your* perspective, approach and style – and in particular its difference from everyone else's – that will provide the rocket fuel to power your idea to the stars? What if your idea will glow with originality just because you for once stopped editing yourself and actually let it all hang out? What would happen if you let *your* light shine?

Our deepest fear is not that we are inadequate. Our deepest fear is that we are powerful beyond measure. It is our light, not our darkness that most frightens us. We ask ourselves, Who am I to be brilliant, gorgeous, talented, fabulous? Actually, who are you not to be? You are a child of God. Your playing small does not serve the world. There is nothing enlightened about shrinking so that other people won't feel insecure around you. We are all meant to shine, as children do. We were born to make manifest the glory of God that is within us. It's not just in some of us; it's in everyone. And as we let our own light shine, we unconsciously give other people permission to do the same. As we are liberated from our own fear, our presence automatically liberates others.

Marianne Williamson, A Return to Love

Austin is America's eleventh biggest city and the state capital of Texas. Founded by pioneers in the 1830s, the city is now a centre of independent thinking, trade and creativity. In the 1990s it was a southern hub for 'slacker' culture and grunge music. In recent years the city has become a hotbed of tech innovation and an international meeting point for independent musicians and filmmakers.

These days Austin has an unofficial motto: 'Keep Austin weird'. Red Wassenich, a librarian in the city, was seeing corporate America eroding Austin's uniqueness and he didn't like it. His request for weirdness was a rallying cry in support of small businesses and indie spirit. It seems to be working – Austin has a thriving local economy and over 19 million people a year visit to experience its unique character.

Weirdness is often good for business, in our experience. A while back, while working with Virgin Atlantic, we found that an extremely large proportion of their customers to whom we spoke spontaneously mentioned the little rubber ducks that were included as a fun gift in their in-flight kits. They loved them. Weird, but true.

Imagine how much it takes to get 400 people and a 367-ton aircraft to fly across the Atlantic. It is an operational task of incredible complexity involving avionics, navigation, hospitality and ticketing. And yet the most frequently mentioned items by ordinary people (i.e. as weird as you and us) that we spoke to were those ducks. A rubber duck won't fill you up when you get hungry or help you sleep better, but in a world of safety briefings and wet-wash serviettes, those ducks stood out. People saw them as iconic of the Virgin Atlantic experience. They represented individuality, generosity and authenticity.

Virgin's priorities are, of course, safety and operational excellence. It takes bravery to commission hundreds of thousands of rubber ducks in that context. On the face of it, those ducks are pointless, but they seem to have created a feeling of comfort, warmth and love in the aircraft. They have certainly become folklore inside Virgin Atlantic. They are a benchmark now for their tone of voice – for staying weird like Austin – and a popular example of how you surprise and delight passengers. More proof that you don't have to be normal (whatever that means) to be successful.

The ducks tell us that innovation isn't only rational. People want to laugh, to feel and to be inspired. As we fill the world with our work, it's our responsibility to do this for our customers. We aren't only here to sell something for more than it costs us. We are creating the world that people live in. Let's aim to make people feel joy as much as part with their money.

With a relatively small and new idea, you have a nearly blank canvas. Why not play a little? Make the most of it! Be a bit weird! No one else can do your idea like you can.

Want to use 10 per cent of your profits to build a donkey sanctuary? Do it!

Want to send a single red rose to every customer? Why not?

Want to give the first customer of the day a hug? Hug away (maybe ask first)!

Want to call your Margherita pizza the 'Marge and Rita'? Do it! No one's going to stop you.

Think the Marge and Rita is a stupid name for a pizza? Think of a better one, then! You're flying this plane . . .

Find your voice

From a branding point of view, finding your own voice is the Holy Grail because it gets you noticed and remembered. By doing what you feel is right, and by using a voice that is your own, you fill your idea with extraordinary energy, and give your users something real to push against. You also differentiate your idea from all others, and set yourself free to have fun.

When Ed Smith and Richard Wilkinson started Doisy & Dam, they realized they weren't just starting a chocolate company – they were starting *their* chocolate company. A seminal moment early in its life showed them the way:

'Before we launched, we went to the Chocolate Expo in Olympia in London. It was all browns and blacks and people were so serious about what they were doing. There's nothing wrong with that – but we walked out of it saying we would never exhibit there. It was so dreary. It helped us realize that we were going to have to be ourselves. We decided that the only way we would create anything interesting was if we used our own tone of voice. And because we've been being ourselves, we have had so much fun making our idea happen.'

Their chocolate company is one of the fastest growing in the UK today. Ed and Richard have done what they feel is right. Their growth hasn't been without its problems, but they have determinedly and successfully found a voice and an approach that has distinguished them from other chocolate brands and inspired a growing band of fans. Ed:

'A brand needs to have an identity in order to be strong – and if you try to fake a tone or fake the way you come across I think everyone's going to see through it. So instead of trying to sound like someone else we decided to do exactly what we would normally do as people. We think people appreciate the sincerity.'

Ed and Richard seem to have systematically broken every chocolate category rule. There are no browns and blacks in Doisy & Dam packaging – just pastel shades and stripes:

'We didn't have the money to pay for a professional designer so I taught myself Illustrator and did the packaging design myself.'

Their flavours are radical too:

'We decided that we wanted to mix superfoods with chocolate, so we've ended up with flavours which are quite different from other chocolates. We've worked out what we think is the perfect combination of flavours . . . and we make sure that every product has a good nutritional profile. I think there's a lot of boring flavours out there – maybe that's because that's the chocolate that people want to buy and we're doing something stupid again, but these are the flavours we love, so that's why we're making them. My favourite flavour at the moment is quinoa, vanilla and lapsang souchong – it's coming out this year.'

Ed and Richard are aware that their voice is as much about what they aren't as what they are:

'To be honest, we've avoided the chocolate world as much as possible. We don't go to trade shows. We love hanging out with start-ups, especially food start-ups. Everyone's doing something different and there's this amazing free sharing of information. We would never get that in the chocolate market which is quite competitive.'

Doisy & Dam have turned being themselves into a business-building strategy. The more they are themselves, the better they seem to do. They're finding their own voice, and having fun – and their idea is becoming so distinct that it's building a loyal following.

Surely, there must be a catch. Surely, you can't just speak your own truth, trust your judgement, call things as you see them and have fun – and expect to see your idea grow. Can you?

Well – yes – there is a catch, as it happens. The catch is that you can't please everyone. By being yourself, you will polarize people. Some people won't like your style.

There is a moment which dramatizes this nicely in the movie *Jerry Maguire*. Tom Cruise plays Jerry, a sports agent who is being squeezed out of his agency by his colleagues. They don't like his style. In a last-ditch attempt to persuade them of his point of view, he stays on late at the office and writes a brand-new mission statement for the business.

He believes this is his moment: he is finally fully representing his point of view, without editing himself. How could they disagree? Surely they will follow him into the future shared in the document he is staying up late to finish.

In the middle of the night, Jerry goes to the copy centre to pick up photocopies of his new mission statement. The copy clerk, having read Jerry's manifesto, hands it to him with the intensity of a believer saying, 'That's how you become great, man – hang your balls out there!'

With the copy clerk's words ringing in his ears, Maguire marches back to the office, and leaves a document on everyone's desk. He is finally letting his light shine. Everyone will surely join him in his enthusiasm when they read his vision for the business.

In the morning, Jerry loses his job. They don't like it.

Being yourself is the ultimate risk. Having a distinct voice will attract fans but it will turn some people off. It takes you somewhere you belong – where you are doing what you believe is right – but the catch is that not everyone will want to join you.

Jerry Maguire's act of self-expression was the end of his relationship with Sports Management International but in the movie it was also the making of him. He was finally free to start making things happen based on his own point of view. He had found his voice. He was – finally – being himself. Sports Management International never 'got' Jerry anyway. Now he was free to find his way in the world, living authentically and making the most of his incredible talents. It is the turning point of the film. Things start getting good for Jerry after that.

Creator story 8: Sharing what you know with the world – childcareisfun.co.uk

Fi Star-Stone worked for many years as a nanny. In that time, she developed a strong sense of how to look after kids – and in particular how to enjoy it. When the mums she met realized this, they would ask her for tips and ideas on a range of parenting subjects such as toilet training, weaning, fussy eating and, the main one, sleep. She sensed that her advice was really helping – in particular she noticed that some of the people she was helping were expressing their deep gratitude.

Realizing that the things she had worked out as a nanny might be useful to a wider audience, she decided to write a blog – childcareisfun.co.uk. She started her website in 2008, intending that it would be a free resource for parents and carers. Very quickly, she started getting email requests for help, so she set up a 'free parent advice service', the first of its kind in the UK.

Fi runs the website herself, inviting her readers to get in touch for advice, because she loves to help. Six years later, she gets around 250 questions a week in her mailbox.

'Sometimes it's parents who are incredibly lonely, sometimes it's people who just need reassurance that they're doing a great job. I love helping people out with what I know – I feel valued and I get incredible feedback. The other day a parent said to me that I had helped her get her life back – she has triplets and got her first good night's sleep in three years!'

She has built quite a following. Her website gets around 50,000 hits a month now and is one of the leading childcare sites. You may have heard about the #twitterbirth of her son Oscar at home on 17 September 2010 which caused quite a stir.

Now, the media are discovering Fi as an expert. She's often invited onto radio and TV shows to give advice to parents – and she's enjoying expanding what she does to more and more people who can benefit from her experience and advice.

Fi regularly writes articles for parenting websites and magazines and she makes a small amount of money from advertising on her site. She has written her first book, *The Baby Bedtime Book*, to help parents get their kids to sleep. It's selling really well, and she is now writing her second.

'I'm not rich, but I'm happy,' says Fi. 'I get a real kick out of helping people all over the world. I just want to show people that childcare needn't be this horrifying experience – it can be fun.'

· how to find an idea like fi did ·

Spot your niche
What do you know about that other people don't? Remember that your area of expertise doesn't need to be huge or popular. The internet means your market is global, so your niche can be small and still have an impact.

Find your own voice
Fi's angle on childcare is that it can be fun. It's what she believes. This gives readers a reason to read, and editors a way of placing Fi in their programming – and it helps Fi with the focus for her writing and opinion pieces.

Be happy giving
In Fi's world, you have to give a lot before you get much back. This is best for people who get a kick out of helping other people, as Fi does.

Network with other experts
There are millions of people who work as information nodes these days, in niches from knitwear to steam engines. Watch them and see how they do it. Techniques in the space tend to be applicable across the full spectrum of niches.

Be proud to be small

There is no need to pretend you're bigger than you are. You don't need to be more experienced, more creative or more business-y either. You don't need to take on anyone else's opinions, attitudes or beliefs. All you have to do is be yourself – all day long, with confidence and in public.

This isn't just us being encouraging. Being yourself is the best business decision you can make. You give your customers something authentic to connect with and you create an idea with energy and originality – that only you can create.

There was a moment very early on – I signed up to Twitter and I had one personal Twitter and another one for Kennedy City Bicycles. Almost immediately I had this thought: why pretend that you're bigger than you are? If you're small, why not have the advantage of being small? Why shouldn't people know they're buying a thing off a person? Why wouldn't you want to talk to the guy who designed it? I closed the Kennedy City Bicycles Twitter down.

James Kennedy, Kennedy City Bicycles

Harriot Pleydell-Bouverie of Mallow and Marsh, tells the story of when she pitched to Sainsbury's as part of a competition among start-ups called PitchUp. The prize was to win a listing in Sainsbury's stores and Harriot had to make a presentation about her product to buyers at the supermarket.

'They asked me how many stores I thought we should be in. I knew that some of the other people pitching had said some pretty big numbers, and I thought there was a risk that I might look too small if I was honest. We were still really small then. We didn't have much of a manufacturing operation. I could have tried to bluff it and said we could manufacture more than we actually could – maybe I could have got away with it and managed to sort it out later – but I decided it was much better to follow my instincts. I was honest and said that we were still small. The team at Sainsbury's said that they loved the fact that I had been realistic and they decided to take my products in a handful of stores.'

Sainsbury's put three variants of Mallow and Marsh marshmallows into forty stores. As Harriot says:

'We wouldn't have been able to cope with much more, and we have been able to grow at the right pace. We are building a great relationship with Sainsbury's based on the reality of our business rather than a fantasy someone thought they wanted to hear.'

When you are a fledgling business, be proud you're new. It is your licence to make mistakes, your launch pad to doing things differently and an invitation to others to help. Honesty has a disarming effect on people. You'll find people want to help you – and because they have the truth about your situation they will be able to help you.

Meanwhile, if you pretend to be someone you're not, you'll get stuck in the problem of working out which story to tell to whom. This is not relaxing. Better to be honest and enjoy the journey. Besides, you won't be small for long.

One of the things that I learned very early on is this: don't try and be bigger than you are. Just be honest and you will be amazed by how much people want to help the little guy and by how accommodating and understanding they are. James Kennedy

Being small is an advantage, rather than something to hide. When Faisel Rahman started Fair Finance he was on his own. He spent the first six months visiting two or three hundred homes a week, meeting people who wanted to borrow money. He wanted to meet the people behind the statistics, to see where they lived, so that he could start to understand what they were like and why they wanted to borrow money.

He knew that his competitors (the banks) had written computer algorithms to save them doing this work, and he had a hunch going door to door would reveal the future of his idea. He was able to look potential customers in the eye and learn who was a good credit risk and who wasn't. Who was going to spend the £500 on a sewing machine, and pay it back once she'd made enough alterations. And who would just vanish into thin air.

In the process, Faisal developed a central insight in Fair Finance's lending policy that has stood to this day – that the key to lending to people with low credit rating was in their friendships. He realized that reliable customers always have friends who will vouch for them personally. This wonderful insight has become a guideline in Fair Finance's lending process:

'So I created a system, a similar one to the one I had seen in the villages back in Bangladesh – one that was focused around trust and people. If you want me to lend you some money when I don't really know you and you don't really know me. So, I tell you what, I'll bring a friend so you can trust my intentions and hear more about me. But then you bring two friends who will vouch for you as a person. Then we'll have a conversation between the five of us and if we all believe that your idea is a good idea then I'll lend you some money.

That's how Fair Finance started and we still use the same system for lending money today.'

Faisel's going from house to house wasn't a 'scaleable solution'. The founder of a growing business like Fair Finance would not always be able to have a cup of tea with every single client, but the information he got from those interactions has been fundamental in how he's structured his entire organization. He now has a feeling for how the system works – because he's met his customers. A smart founder does this while he can – while his idea is still small – since he knows that when he has 10,000 or 100,000 customers he won't be able to.

Fair Finance has now been going for fourteen years, and makes nearly 10,000 loans a year. It was one of the Big Society award winners in 2013. Faisel has revolutionized access to capital for the socially excluded in the UK and changed how we look at debt – and it all started with him having cups of tea with prospective clients – when he saw being small as an advantage rather than something to hide.

Find out more about Faisel's story at theideainyou.com.

Iconic actions

You have an enormous amount of freedom in deciding how you want to do things. We can think of only three universal rules: your idea must be legal, it must offer value and it must ultimately bring in more money than you spend. Beyond that you can be as weird as you like.

All the choices you make – including where you work, how you make your product, how you conduct your relationships with suppliers and employers and partners and how you decide to structure your organization – combine to make your idea. It's not just your idea – it's also the systems and structures you build that define what happens and how people will respond to you.

The more you can make choices which align with your own values, and take decisions to do things the way you want to do them rather than just modelling those who have come this way before you, the more you will distinguish your idea from everyone else's.

This is how you build a brand. More than just what you say or what you look like, more than just logos, designs and advertising and tone of voice – your brand is born from the inner workings of your idea. It is derived from the things you do.

Everything you do – both internal and external, both visible and invisible – combines into the impact your idea has on the world. You shape the final outcome in all the little things you do.

Because they're fundamental to how your idea works and how it's perceived, we call such activities *iconic actions*.

Iconic actions – Where you work

Paul started parkrun from a shed at the end of his garden. This kept him in his community and near his family – both important parts of the parkrun ethos. Now there is a pattern emerging in the leaders of parkrun, as it rolls out globally. Tom Williams, head of parkrun UK, has built an identical shed at the bottom of his garden.

This works for parkrun. What would work for you? Where would you like to work? Why? You decide.

Iconic actions – How you make your product

Ed and Richard from Doisy & Dam received advice from a friendly contact (a manufacturing expert who had recently sold his ethical beverage company to a multinational for £100m) that they should outsource the manufacturing of their chocolate. Instead, Ed and Richard decided to do it themselves, and found their own chocolatier. This meant creating every element of their product, even though they realized that this was *'like starting an airline and ignoring Richard Branson's advice'*.

'Doing something physical, productive and constructive is what we love doing. It's still painful doing it but it's been so fulfilling. There's personal pride in it – we make our own chocolate. Our friend was right – I'm sure half the things we've done have been mistakes and it's been painful – but we wouldn't go back.'

This works for Doisy & Dam. How are you going to 'manufacture' your idea? What choices do you have – and how important are they? You decide.

Iconic actions – How you work with suppliers

Thom and James from Pizza Pilgrims are developing a limoncello – an Italian liqueur made with lemons. On their travels in Italy they have found a supplier they love, who has a grove full of delicious lemons. Many people would just make a phone call and buy some fruit. Not Thom and James. Instead of phoning in their order, they have asked if they can come over and help pick them from the trees.

'It's an adventure. It's fun! We want to see where they grow, smell them as we pick them, meet the people who have grown them. We can also film it and it makes great content for our website.'

This works for Thom and James. How are you going to make the most of the relationships you build around your idea? You decide.

Iconic actions – Which partners you work with (and which you don't)

The people you partner with will become part of the culture around your idea. You get to pick who these are. You can move towards the people you believe will add to the culture, and quietly step away from those you don't. Over time, you will create relationships you care about and which feel right to you.

Doisy & Dam are very much aware of the retailers they sell through, and are developing a point of view about who they want to work with and who they don't:

'We started by selling into independent shops in London. They were great to take us on. We had no proven history of sales. Our packaging was totally

illegal but they took us on anyway. Since then, we've gone into some much larger places, and we've made sure we've stayed in touch with them.'

When we met Ed and Richard, though, their originality and energy had taken them to a new level, exposing them to a range of new possible relationships. One in particular is making them question how they want their relationships to work. Richard:

'There are a few national supermarket chains which take advantage of their size – you can guess who we are talking about. They ask you to pay listing fees. You have to pay them £2,000 per product just to be on their shelves. It feels wrong that we have to not only prove the quality of our product but also pay for the pleasure of being sold. They don't even seem to care about the product. They will drop you if you don't pay. We are coming to the conclusion that we would rather not have the sales than feel like someone is blackmailing us into a sales opportunity. I have no idea whether this is the right decision from a business point of view but we are probably going to say no to them.'

This works for Doisy & Dam. What kind of partners will *you* want to work with? Who is right for you and your idea? You decide.

Iconic actions – How you structure your business

In 2009 Mark Johnson, an ex-offender and entrepreneur, started User Voice, a charitable organization consulting directly with prisoners to understand what help they need and facilitating their dialogue with prison governors. It also provides support and employment opportunities for ex-offenders when they leave prison. User Voice is active in prisons up and down the country. It has helped shape government policy on how to rehabilitate inmates, and changed the lives of hundreds of offenders and ex-offenders.

But when Mark started User Voice he was creating more than just an organization that would help ex-offenders like him. He was trying to replicate the conditions that had helped him turn his life round:

'It's all about ownership. When I started my tree surgery business straight after leaving prison it was the best form of rehab back into the world. I couldn't blame anyone. I had to front up and take ownership for my actions

and my life. It forced me to learn what being a functioning human being meant again after seven years of living on the street in London and nearly two decades of heroin addiction.'

Mark has carried this principle through to how he structures User Voice internally.

'It makes me smile when ex-offenders walk in here on their first day out of prison and say, "What are you going to do for me?" I say, "What are you going to do for yourself?" User Voice is set up to be run by them, by ex-offenders.'

Mark designs management structures in such a way that ex-offenders have to take ownership and get involved; they can't lean back and pass responsibility to someone else.

Mark believes in the power of ownership to the extent that he's created a company that he doesn't run.

This works for User Voice. How will you structure your idea, so that it creates the right dynamics for success and how you want it to work? You decide.

Iconic actions – Who you hire

Kathryn Parsons runs Decoded. Decoded's goal is to help non-digital people develop an enthusiastic appreciation and understanding of the digital world. Decoded call it 'digital enlightenment' – and it is exemplified by its signature course, 'Code_in a Day.'

Hiring people into Decoded as they expand internationally has been one of Kathryn's biggest challenges:

'We had been trying to make sure that people's experience matched what we wanted them to do, and we were finding it really hard to find good people. Eventually, it dawned on us that we were good judges of character, so we started backing ourselves, and simply asking ourselves, "Is this person amazing? Do they have emotional intelligence? Will people enjoy working with them?" Then things got really good. We were hiring for talent and attitude more than simply experience – and we're great judges of that when we meet people. It makes Decoded a fantastic place to work. The team really are fascinating, amazing people – passionate, respectful, interesting people. It's what I am most proud of.'

This works for Decoded. How would you think about the people you want to work with? How would you find them? You decide.

Iconic actions – The goals you focus on

At Decoded, Kathryn has realized that their best measure of success is genuine digital enlightenment:

'We have been asking for ratings from clients who have done our courses and we have consistently got good scores, so we decided to raise the bar. Now our most useful measure of success is how many of our clients agree that we changed their life. We're not just trying to fill gaps in people's learning – we want them to experience the world differently after they've spent time with us.'

How are you going to know if you are doing well? What are your measures of success? You decide.

Iconic actions – Who does which jobs

Whatever your work history before now, you can now fill whichever roles you want at your idea. It may seem appropriate to do the work you know well, but there are advantages to following your nose into the work that you are newly drawn to. Ed and Richard from Doisy & Dam have had this experience:

'We both wanted to do the things we enjoy. We both wanted to decide what packaging we use and we both wanted to go to the sales meetings. When we did our first hire we made sure that she did every aspect of the business too so that she could fall into an area that she enjoyed. It turns out that she's brilliant at product development. If we'd got her in and said, "You can do our accounts," she'd probably have left within three months. Instead she's really enjoying herself and bringing loads of value to the business. She's also got a much better understanding of how our business works. We want to do that with everyone we hire – so that people get a good all-round view of how the business works.'

This works for Doisy & Dam. How are you going to distribute the tasks necessary to realize your idea? If you're on your own, this one's easy. If you're not – what's your point of view? What will be the impact on the future of your idea if you share the tasks around so that people learn more? What will be the impact if you use only specialists? You decide.

Iconic actions – What you call your idea

You'll be saying it a lot, and so will other people, so pick a name you care about.

Charlie of Run Dem Crew:

'We decided we're going to call it a Crew, not a club, because club sounds old-fashioned, and we're going to call it the craziest name we can find, so that when you look down the race results and you're seeing the Beagles and the Harriers and whatever and then you see Run Dem Crew, you're going to think, "Who's that?!"'

Ed and Richard from Doisy & Dam decided to call their idea after two Nobel prize winners who discovered Vitamin K:

'Doisy & Dam did a lot of the important early work into nutrition – and it felt right to call our business after them. It's also completely different from every other chocolate bar.'

This works for Run Dem Crew and Doisy & Dam. How can you make the name of your idea iconic? You decide.

· DO IT NOW ·
develop iconic actions

By now, we hope you've got a concept, a dream, a *why*, and a product in development. You've put your Version Zero out into the world and you are in a feedback loop, learning how to improve it.

Now it's time to start thinking about what is distinct in the internal and external decisions you make about how you run your idea. It's time to reflect on your *iconic actions*.

continued

The right iconic actions for you will help you deliver against your *why* – your idea's ideology – and will help you meet the promises in your concept. They are steps on the road to the *dream* for your idea.

Feel free to 'model', to borrow ideas from people you meet and the stories you've read here, but make sure they work for you. Over time you will develop a set of iconic actions that works for you and your idea and which are different from everyone else's.

You will find it easiest to develop these choices over time, so don't worry if your iconic actions aren't completely obvious to you now. It is worth reflecting on how you think you want to do things now, however. It's also worth giving yourself permission to stay a little weird like Austin.

In time these iconic actions will create a unique idea aligned with your own values. You can enjoy making it happen and delight in the change it makes in the world.

Consider a range of iconic actions:

- Where you work.
- The materials, processes and suppliers you use to make your idea.
- Your working partners and how you want to work with them.
- How you structure the organization around your idea.
- The goals you focus on.
- How you answer the phone, what's in your email footer and how you describe yourself in your Twitter profile.

If you think about it, every action is iconic. Trust your instincts and do what you think is right and your idea will stand out as something truly original.

To be yourself in a world that is constantly trying to make you something else is the greatest accomplishment.

Ralph Waldo Emerson

NEVER, EVER GIVE UP

A good half of the art of living is resilience.

Alain de Botton, writer and philosopher

Mark Johnson took heroin for the first time in the winter of 1981. He was eleven.

'I lived on the streets of London for seven years with hardly any possessions and a £400-a-day heroin addiction. My habit took everything from me, and nearly my life – and at the time I wished it had. I saw others die and I did things to survive that would shock most people.'

After fifteen years of addiction, Mark got himself into rehab and began to reflect on his life.

'I asked myself, what good could possibly have come from those years? I couldn't think at that point, so I wrote: pages and pages of notes, filling a stack of black diaries. By the time I finished writing, I was starting to look at my "wasted" years differently. At the peak of my addiction, I was finding a way to get hold of £400 in cash a day in the fastest possible time. I was always 100 per cent focused on the task at hand. I would let nothing deter me from getting what I needed to feed my addiction. I was in service to my addiction night and day and would walk miles on end to get what I needed. I overcame everything – no matter how hard, unpleasant or terrifying it was.'

In 2009, Mark founded User Voice, a charitable organization

facilitating dialogue between prisoners and prison governors. An ex-offender, almost twenty-year heroin addict – who thought he had nothing – went back into prison as an ex-offender and created a new conversation. Barry Greenberry, former Governor of HMP Isle of Wight, described it as 'one of the most effective and inspiring things I have ever seen in prison'.

A last word from Mark:

'My years of addiction had taught me more than I thought. They had shown me how to be resilient. That's what everything in life comes down to. Resilience.'

If you have read this far, you have already come a long way. You have shown that you have a hunger to change your life. You have demonstrated the willingness to commit time and energy to your journey. If you have been doing the '**DO IT NOW**' exercises throughout the book, you have also shown the resourcefulness and energy that you will need in spades over the coming months and years.

But, it is unlikely that your resilience has been tested yet. Not properly. We don't like to be overly pessimistic, but we can say with some confidence that this will change.

As you put your idea out into the world, you will be challenged. Things will go wrong. You will encounter uncertainty and failure – probably many times.

When you start making your idea happen, you find yourself in this weird place of uncertainty. Before this, in your day job, you knew exactly what you were doing. Now everything is new. And you are making mistakes. Lots of them. It's a massive change that no one tells you about when you are starting out.   Thom Elliot, Pizza Pilgrims

We have dedicated much of this book to the mental game of making your idea happen: how you think, what your awareness is of yourself and what you are going through. This is crucial to the process. And when things get hard, it gets more important.

Even though we all dream about growing our ideas, the irony is that the more your idea grows, the bigger the challenge becomes.

As your idea becomes more visible, the stakes get higher. You have more to do, more feedback from the world, more opportunity, more challenge. Resilience becomes more and more important. To give you an idea of why it's good to build your resilience before it's required, here are some scenarios that the creators we met have faced as they have built their ideas. We're not trying to scare you – just prepare you!

- A blogger denounces your idea, using their public platform to go into great detail on why it's not to be trusted. A major newspaper fans the flames by linking to the blog piece.
- A large retailer demands that you pay a listing fee and reduce your profit margin if they are to continue to stock your product.
- A friend decides just before launch that they don't want to be a partner with you on your idea after all. They go back to their day job, leaving you to build it on your own.
- One of your first employees turns out to be a bad fit. You have to let them go. They don't like it.
- You receive an offer of investment. It will take away all your immediate problems but the vision of the investor is a little different from yours. What do you do?
- You get flu but have scheduled a week of new business discussions overseas that could transform your business.
- The first delivery of hundreds of your new product looks great, but the supplier has put the wrong labels on.

All the creators we spoke to felt genuinely tested by these scenarios – but they found a way to keep going. They practised resilience. The good news is that resilience is something all of us can develop.

Where resilience comes from

When we tackle obstacles, we find hidden reserves of courage and resilience we did not know we had. And it is only when we are faced with failure do we realize that these resources were always there within us. We only need to find them.

A. P. J. Abdul Kalam, writer and former President of India.

On 4 August 2010, at the San Jose copper-gold mine in Chile, miners clambered on board dumper trucks and rode down spiralling service ramps to a depth of 700 metres. A mix of hardy old pros and technical support personnel with little underground mining experience, they were in good spirits that day, laughing and cracking jokes. For many of them, this was to be the beginning of an extraordinary experience.

At 1 p.m. that afternoon, a block of granite as tall as a forty-five-storey building broke loose and crashed through the many warren-like layers of the mine, sealing the miners in beneath 770,000 tons of rock. They would be there for sixty-nine days.

After the frantic early hours trying to find an escape route and compiling resources, an epic test began. For those of us who want to learn how to keep going in the face of the relatively minor difficulties and failures involved in making an idea happen, those miners – and one in particular – can teach us a lot.

It wasn't until 22 August 2010 – seventeen days after the rockfall – that the miners even connected with the outside world. A rescue drill bit penetrated their refuge in the depths – and when it rose back up to the surface it had the words *Estamos bien en el refugio, los 33* – literally, *We are well in the shelter, the 33 of us* – taped to it.

The message made its way via the assembled media to an audience of billions, offering hope to their families and fuelling a story which ran and ran on news shows. Meanwhile, amidst all the relief, 'Los 33' were still faced with the very real prospect of a slow death in a tomb of rock 700 metres beneath the Atacama desert.

Mario Sepulveda, a forty-year-old father of two, would emerge as an inspirational leader for the group. It wasn't his age or rank that afforded him this position – he wasn't one of the senior members of the crew – it was his *attitude* in the face of the uncertainty facing the group.

His determination and infectious optimism were there for the world to see at his rescue when, after more than two months underground, he emerged blinking from the depths and whipped the waiting crowds into a frenzy with fevered cries of *'Viva Chile!'*

It turns out that Mario had known adversity before. His mother had died giving birth to him and his life had been characterized by poverty and occasional violence. He had become accustomed to fighting to stay alive. Life had taught Mario to be resilient. He had learned to expect survival through a life of genuine hardship. Even if you are lucky enough to have had a life so far in which your resilience hasn't been tested like it was in Mario's, his story shows us that resilience can be *learned*.

Creator story 9: Be the person who does what everyone else is thinking – Decoded

Kathryn Parsons knew there was a need for someone to demystify the digital world because she felt it herself. She was running a digital consultancy and realized she wanted to know more about the language behind what she was doing. 'I could see code was changing how the world worked, and I wanted to understand it better than I did. I had a hunch that many other people would too.'

Kathryn had found something universal. A rapid change in technology had created a gap in knowledge for a large number of people. In 2011 she started Decoded – a training business specializing in 'digital enlightenment'. Her goal was to teach anyone to 'Code in a Day'.

Kathryn's idea has grown very quickly. Decoded is now a diverse team, with a stated mission of demystifying the digital world. They have already taken their 'learning experiences' to thirty-five cities around the world and are now expanding their curriculum to include hacking, digital leadership and the Internet of Things.

· how to do what kathryn did ·

Work out your why
Decoded know why they want to train people. DEMYSTIFYING THE DIGITAL WORLD is written (in capitals) across the front page of their website. This is what Kathryn felt she needed when she started Decoded – and now her idea is doing this for a global audience.

continued

How to up your resilience

Resilience is how you respond to problems. It is not a singular response, it is a mindset – a number of different attributes that combine and help us to overcome challenges that we never thought possible. We can practise each one.

Breaking out these attributes and focusing on them one at a time will eventually increase your resilience and help you to overcome whatever crosses your path.

1. Be positive

In the situation the miners were in, there were many reasons why they might die, but Mario Sepulveda looked for why they would live. In the mine, moments after the collapse, the miners did a head count, and realized there were thirty-three of them down there. Mario's first response was: *'Thirty-three! The age of Christ! Shit! . . . This has to mean something. There's something bigger for us waiting outside.'*

His speech to the group struck a deep and lasting chord with his colleagues, and provided them with new resolve and strength.

Positive thoughts trigger positive emotions. Staying positive like this is the foundation of resilience. If your thoughts become negative, your emotions will follow, and your actions will be next.

In the life of your idea, you will have choices about how you respond to your circumstances. There will, of course, be moments when news comes in which isn't ideal, and when you sense that this task is harder than you thought it would be. This is a moment when you can test your capacity for looking on the bright side. Be conscious of how you react to adversity. Like Mario, take the decision to view things from a positive perspective. Count your blessings. Focus on the good news you have. It will help you through your darkest hours.

2. Treat difficult moments as turning points

'The only thing I do is live!'

These were Mario Sepulveda's first words in the moments after the catastrophic rockfall in the San Jose mine.

You will encounter joy and success, but you can expect to stumble from time to time too. Failure and disappointment are part of all our stories. We can't completely avoid them; but we can control how we respond.

Our efforts to get this book published included a moment that transformed the way we think about resilience. The first meeting we had with a publisher went extremely well for us. They said they really liked the book. They even gave us a date when they thought it would be good to release it. We practically rolled out of the meeting, backslapping each other and congratulating ourselves, certain we had sealed the deal – and from our first ever publisher meeting too.

A week later we received an email from the same publisher. It included a resounding 'no' and some feedback, including the following withering advice: 'I think their proposal and vision needs work, I'm afraid, especially the title and subtitle and overall premise.' In other words: rethink the whole thing.

We felt ashamed and we were worried that we had just learned that it takes more than we had to give to get a book published in this arena. We had been overconfident and underprepared.

After we'd licked our wounds for a while, it dawned on us that we had two ways of responding. We could crumble, or we could see this as a turning point. That tough feedback had taught us something vital – in fact, it was a priceless gift to us. We needed to be better prepared next time, and much clearer about the book we wanted to write.

We looked into every point in the feedback and put a plan into action to deal with each one. We had the email from that first publisher meeting on a piece of paper in front of us as we rehearsed what we were going to say in our next. We worked hard.

The next meeting we had was with Penguin Portfolio. A week later we had a deal.

Every moment of failure is a potential turning point. If you focus on the opportunity for change it offers, you make the most of it. The fact you are holding this book in your hands is testament to this.

The greatest glory in living lies not in never falling, but in rising every time we fall. Nelson Mandela

3. Be in the service of something bigger than you

Faithless is he that says farewell when the road darkens.
J. R. R. Tolkien, *The Fellowship of the Ring*

In times of adversity, it is often a higher faith or goal that survivors cite as the source of their strength. For many of the Chilean miners it was faith in God. For others it was their desire to get home to their families.

As you develop your idea, you can draw resilience from being in service of something bigger than your own success or achievements. Your idea will change the world, not just your own life. When times get hard, return to the source of strength in your *why*, to the meaning your idea has for you, and use it as fuel to keep going.

This is one of the reasons we have encouraged you to explore the meaning you want from your idea, and its *why*. These things will strengthen your resolve in hard times.

4. Get help

We human beings are social beings. We come into the world as the result of others' actions. We survive here in dependence on others. Whether we like it or not, there is hardly a moment of our lives when we do not benefit from others' activities. For this reason, it is hardly surprising that most of our happiness arises in the context of our relationships with others.   The Dalai Lama

In practice when we set out on a new journey of bringing an idea to life, many of us leave behind a busy office and people to talk to. More often than not we replace it with a kitchen table, a laptop and just a radio DJ for company. By becoming a creator, we 'go it alone'. With our focus so strongly on what we want to achieve we fail to see the social structures we are discarding, and as His Holiness the Dalai Lama reminds us, 'most of our happiness arises in the context of our relationships with others'.

Relationships are a supercharger for resilience. We get a helping hand, a shoulder to cry on and someone to celebrate with. As a creator, it's sensible to think about how you will have these even after you no longer have a canteen, water cooler or photocopier. Here are our suggestions for having help on hand when you need it:

Create virtual partnerships
Harriot from Mallow and Marsh doesn't have a partner in her business, but has found a different way of getting company, support and skills from others:

'Knowing myself, I think it's good I don't have a business partner, but I've created a group of people who have become really good friends, who are all running small food businesses. They know what I'm going through and

they're like business partners too – I can call on them, depending what they're speciality is. It's about surrounding yourself with people who get it – and no one gets working twenty-four hours a day, seven days a week like someone else who is doing that. It's networking but on a friendship level. If something's going wrong, they're the people who I'll call up. They're also the people who I celebrate with.'

Build a virtual board

Ed and Richard at Doisy & Dam made an active decision to create a *board* of helpers early in the development of their chocolate company. Comprising people they already knew who have the experience Ed and Rich didn't yet have, this is an elite group:

'We drew on our resources – people we knew who had different experiences in business. Some entrepreneurial, some larger retail based, some finance based – all these different things where everyone had a bit of advice to give us. We still have that group of people. They're like a non-exec board. We pay them with chocolate. We usually buy them a beer or buy them lunch or something like that. Colin Fenn from Fenn Wright Manson, David Krantz, who built Racing Green and Blazer, Adam Balon from Innocent. A lot of the advice has been fantastic and it's one of the reasons why we are here today.'

We don't all have an address book like Ed and Rich's but we all know people who know more than we do, people who themselves will have benefited from what we describe in the next chapter as the Economy of Favours. They will have received help from people as they were learning, and now they may be prepared to help you. If you don't ask – how will they know you need it?

Find a partner

Many choose to make this journey with someone else. Two heads are better than one, of course, and with the right partner, the journey can also be more fun.

You actually notice it more in the good times than the bad times. Having someone who is in it with you to share the great moments and successes.

When we got the keys to our first pizzeria James and I went in to have a celebratory beer together and ended up leaving at 4 a.m. Those are the moments that make the journey.   Thom Elliot

If you're inclined to find a partner, you may not have to look far. Zach Klein, who started Vimeo in 2004, suggests you probably know them already:

'If you're looking for a partner, you've probably already met them. In our lifetime we make thousands of decisions that lead us to this particular time and place and it's not random that the people sitting around you are there. They've also made similar decisions. These are people we are more likely to be able to trust and resonate with. If you are not in your life surrounded by people that you're resonating with, then I bet there are some decisions that you haven't made because you're afraid. If there's some place that you need to go, or something you need to do – you should do it. Because going to those places and doing those things will likely lead you to the people with whom you feel most comfortable.'

But how do you know a partner when you see one? We believe you are looking for three things:

- *Complementary skills*: Someone who will enjoy hoovering up the tasks you feel least comfortable doing, and who loves having you around because you're good at what they find hard.
- *Character*: Someone who will keep going – and will help you keep going. Make sure that you've spent time together and been through a few challenging experiences with your new partner before you start sharing your business with them. Spend time together and learn how well you work. Create something together which stretches you; spend a few weekends camping and hillwalking; climb a mountain. Make sure that you've seen each other at your worst as well as your best.
- *Commitment*: Check what your partner is expecting from the next few years. There are going to be ups and downs. Are they really IN, or are they going to bolt once something better comes along? Actions are more reliable than words here, so spend time with them and develop some of your idea together, just to

get a feel for their level of commitment. Have a think about what they are usually like with commitment too. Do they commit to their friends, or their other projects? If they are the type to stay in the game, they're welcome on your team.

In any case, take your time before you agree the terms on any partnership. With the right partner, because it will be so obvious it's working, there will be no hurry to lock down any terms.

5. Whatever you do – look after yourself

Take care of your damn teeth!

> Patti Smith, poet, singer, philosopher in her
> Pratt Institute commencement address

If you're feeling well, you'll be resilient. If you're hungover, unfit or needing root canal work, you'll struggle.

When in your life have you felt at your peak? When did you feel you could take on anything that came your way? When have you been the most invincible – the most resilient? The chances are it wasn't after a big night out or a week of overeating. We're guessing it was when you were feeling good – when you had been eating and sleeping well.

Looking after yourself strengthens your resilience. It increases your ability to respond positively to whatever happens. Take control of your physical health: it supports your mental health and your emotional wellbeing. Good health increases the chances of you making your idea happen, and enjoying it.

How to do this without joining the gym:

Work out your own formula for health

- How much sleep do you need to feel good?
- How much food to stay at a healthy weight? How much exercise to feel strong?
- How much company, fresh air, fun and relaxation?
- Listen to your body and your emotions and work out what *you*

need to stay well. This is a personal thing. Forget what everyone else needs. There is no reason your formula should be the same as anyone else's. If you need eight hours of sleep, make sure you get it.

Go outside
Spending twenty minutes outdoors in good weather helps with creative thinking and gets you twenty minutes of fresh air. It gets you away from your work and your computer – and, we believe, builds resilience.

Keep up hobbies
Your photography, snooker, improv classes, baking and biking will provide balance in your life and refresh your mental and physical energy levels. Great for resilience.

Spend time with people you enjoy
A sense of humour helps your resilience. Hanging out with people who make you happy is a free, fun and easy way to stay mentally and emotionally strong, and make light of situations.

Treat yourself
Cook yourself a nice meal, go on a weekend break, go for a beauty treatment, see an old friend. Whatever it is, in the words of the song, 'Enjoy Yourself (It's Later Than You Think)'.

eleven

THE ECONOMY OF FAVOURS

It is literally true that you can succeed best and quickest by helping others to succeed. Napoleon Hill, author of *Think and Grow Rich*

We grew up thinking business was a competition. We'd seen *Wall Street* and done 'competitor analysis' for our clients, and read in the newspaper business sections about big companies 'losing share' to other big companies. Here, we thought, was a world with winners and losers. To get your share, you needed to be smarter or bolder than the other guy.

There is an assumption of scarcity in that way of looking at the world. It imagines that there is a finite pool of money or customers available – and implies a competition to get your share. It's as if there is a limited number of customers to go round, and you have to fight other companies for them if you want to win.

If you see the world like this, it makes sense to keep what you know close to your chest, and to resist helping other people. You don't want other businesses knowing what you do – they'll eat your lunch.

When we spoke to creators, though, we found a different ethic at work. They were focused on making their ideas useful and valuable, of course, but they wanted other creators to do this too. They were sharing what they had learned. They were helping each other, even their competitors in some cases. This from James Kennedy, creator of Kennedy City Bicycles:

'When I first started out, a local bike shop I really like asked me for help with supplies. I had good contacts in Taiwan and I could get bike parts sent here fairly cheaply. I got various parts sent over and passed them on at cost price. There wasn't really an obvious benefit to me of doing that, apart from being nice. They are good people and it felt right.

'Anyway, as it turns out they have a railway arch with lots of space in it. My issue is storage – and now I have a hundred bike frames sitting in their railway arch – because he said, "Why not – we're not using it!" '

The story continues . . .

'I go away on my honeymoon soon for four weeks – and they're going to build all my bikes for me for free while I'm away. Our relationship with each other is brilliant – it feels awesome knowing that we have the ability to help each other and in the most practical sense giving things to each other is much cheaper than buying them off each other.'

We saw this kind of thing a lot. Creators tend to help each other. They assume *abundance*. They take the view that there will be enough to go round for all of us so we can afford to share.

When we assume abundance like this (as opposed to scarcity), we create space in our lives to help each other. We get to enjoy the benefits of each other's experience too, and we get the satisfaction of seeing the whole picture expand rather than just our small part of it.

We call this the Economy of Favours.

This is an economy where the supply of its principal currency – help – is practically infinite.

It's underpinned by two simple guiding principles:

1. *Give unconditionally* – because you want to help.
2. *Ask for help when you need it* – there is a community of people just like you out there who know how hard what you're doing is.

As James's story highlights, helping each other is more than just the right thing to do from a moral perspective, or just something that feels good, it also makes good business sense.

Give and take

Life's most persistent and urgent question is, 'What are you doing for others?' Martin Luther King

Imagine the development of your idea as a series of rungs on a ladder. You start on the ground and climb one rung at a time, each one representing a new learning phase as you grow your idea. When you step onto a new rung, you take on challenges you haven't encountered before – new markets, new technologies, new techniques.

Up ahead of you on the ladder are people who have already done what you're now doing for the first time. If you want help, you can look up the ladder. From time to time, if the system works, the people up there will look down and try to help you up.

I think it's great when companies are prepared to do the sharing part – and are open about their learning. If people don't have to learn the hard way, all the better. I think I benefit from giving back too, because it reminds me of the lessons I have already learned.

Harriot Pleydell-Bouverie,
Mallow and Marsh

The Economy of Favours is a virtuous circle dependent on our ability to give what we have learned unconditionally. We get value back because we give without expectation. It's a curious dynamic but it seems to work. One possible explanation is that acts of unconditional generosity are often paid back in even greater measure than the original act itself. Robert Cialdini, in his book *Influence: The Psychology of Persuasion*, calls this *reciprocity*. When we are given something by somebody else, we can't help but feel the urge to return the favour.

And so the ladder of reciprocity unfolds – ad infinitum. You can give help, so you offer it. You need help, so you ask. Business goes in cycles like this. You go from knowing what you're doing, to taking a step up to a new phase of fresh challenges. You switch from being someone who needs help to someone who has the space to offer it – and back again.

By being someone who both gives and takes in this economy, you feed the virtuous circle within it. Think of it like an ecosystem. It needs feeding, and it needs purpose, so when you take, remember to give some day – and when you give, feel good when you take some day.

Here are four ways that you can quickly and easily help others in the Economy of Favours (you may also see what you need in this list):

1. Offer encouragement

Encouragement requires no experience. You'd be surprised by how many people close to a new creator find it difficult to offer encouragement. All it takes is interest, some generosity of spirit and a few kind words. Simple but powerful stuff.

2. Offer your time

You may not have relevant expertise to offer but a pair of helping hands can make a big difference. Being there for someone when they need it most on their journey, whether it is to lick envelopes, or mentor someone you think you can help, is an act of generosity that will create momentum in the Economy of Favours.

3. Offer your skills

Dig around in your kitbag. What have you got? Customer service expertise? Ideas for promotions? Social media wizardry? Design? The dark arts of Microsoft Excel? You have plenty to offer – share it! The internet is a great place to do this if you prefer staying at home. Write a blog showing how you solved a problem – or write a book like we did.

4. Share your story

Stories help people. They offer colour and detail. Share your hard-won stories with others – at events and conferences, say. It's good for business too, because people will learn about you and what you're doing with your idea.

Resources freely available to you

As a creator, you should also know that there is a lot of help available. As far as your government is concerned, you are on your way to being someone who will employ people, who will pay corporation tax and who will boost your country's exports. They are keen to help.

Viviane Jaeger and Emma-Jayne Parkes are two people who have learned to make the most of the help available. They met while they were studying at London College of Fashion. Their idea has forced them to understand the worlds of intellectual property, chemistry and manufacturing.

Now, through their business SquidLondon, they design and sell Squidarellas. Squidarellas are umbrellas which transform from monochrome to multi-coloured when it rains. When we met them, they were developing a special one for theatre company Cirque du Soleil, and managing orders for their range from retailers around the world.

Emma-Jayne and Viviane had to develop an understanding of intellectual property law and manufacturing as well as the aesthetics and functionality of kids' clothes and umbrellas. They even developed an ink solution which they have been able to patent. They don't teach you how to do this stuff at fashion college.

Notably, Emma-Jayne and Viviane built a relationship with the Business and IP Centre at the British Library. The friendly people at the Library are particularly focused on helping start-ups. Emma-Jayne and Viviane were able to develop a good understanding of the markets they were getting into and the intellectual property position of their products, just by trawling its huge range of market research, company data, patent indexes and statistics. All of these services were and remain completely free.

For more information on the British Library Business and IP Centre, check out Section 3 of the Creator's Black Book (p. 197) or visit theideainyou.com.

How to be a good citizen in the Economy of Favours

The Economy of Favours is kept alive by a respect for other people's time and energy. Creators tend to be busy people, so the clarity of our conversations, both as helper and helped, is important. We don't want to waste each other's time.

There is a technique you can use in this context to keep interactions crisp and purposeful. We thank ?What If! Innovation, the company where we met and started working together, for our knowledge of this technique. They are probably the most insightful business in the world on the *how* of innovation. They have created huge change in the cultures and product portfolios of some of the most successful businesses in the world. One of the techniques they use to great effect is called signalling. Signalling has oiled the wheels of thousands of their interactions – by making them efficient, clear and utterly respectful of each other's time and energy.

It's simple, but it's staggering how often people who are working together don't do it.

Here's how it works. There are just two steps:

1. Before you speak, think about what you want from the conversation that you're about to begin. What are you hoping to get from it? How will you know when you've got it?
2. Now, once you know this as specifically as possible, tell your collaborator(s) so they know too. Now they can give you what you need. No wasted time or energy – just utter clarity of purpose.

Imagine you want to share an idea you've had with a friend. Your first instinct may be to say 'Hey! Look at my idea! What do you think?' – but stop. If you're going to signal well, first you need to have a deeper think about what you need in order that you can tell them.

Get specific. Do you want help with the name or with developing the way your idea could work operationally or with how you communicate its benefits or with developing your thinking about how it makes money? Work it out – and then tell them. If you don't, you're involving them in a long conversation to help you work out what you want. If you do, you make the most of the time you both have because you know what you need – and now they know too.

There is a wide range of conversation types you might signal to another creator. So long as you know what you want or can offer, you can signal the need for

- a decision-making conversation (we need to make a decision!);
- a chat about process (how are we going to approach this problem? We can talk about the content of the problem once we've got the process worked out);
- a 'clear the air' conversation (we've been having problems but now we need to move on);
- a discussion about principles (let's talk about what sorts of things we are going to do before we actually get into the detail);
- a chance to get something off your chest;
- the opportunity to have fun bouncing what you're thinking off someone and just see where it goes;
- or even a shoulder to cry on.

Experts at signalling have almost a sixth sense about where a conversation is going, and how to take it where they think it needs to go. Conversations for fun, which meander casually, still have their place. There's no need to signal then, unless you want to. But when time is tight, and you are asking for or offering help in the delicate Economy of Favours, try signalling instead. You'll keep the virtuous circle turning – and we all benefit from that.

There is more help for you too

For the times when you don't know who to ask for help, or just when you need some inspiration, support or advice please come and join the free Creator Community at theideainyou.com.

We offer help on there: webinars, creator interviews and resources, and there's a forum to seek advice and meet other creators. It's there for you when you need it – perhaps when you just want to get out of your own idea for a while and into someone else's. You can also share the story of your idea and what you've learned along the way.

There is also, over the next several pages, a stage-by-stage list of resources, most of which are free. Stand by.

· DO IT NOW ·
step into the economy of favours

Find and connect with someone who can help you.

They may be a couple of rungs ahead of you on the ladder, and able to help you understand more about what to do – or they may be at the same stage and you will be able to swap stories about what works.

Connect by email or LinkedIn and – remember – *signalling* will help here. You might try something like this:

Hi my name is xxx, I am developing an idea which is (insert your idea and your why) . . .

I hope it is OK to contact you – I just wanted to get in touch because I really like what you are doing and I wanted to [swap advice / get your advice].

In particular, I would love to know a bit about how you solved the problem of [insert what you want to know here as specifically as possible].

Start a conversation with someone. It may lead somewhere extraordinary. Even if it doesn't, you are getting used to the fundamentals of this economy: it will give you all the help you need.

You can do this

We hope that this book has shown you that you will succeed. You – just as you are now. Not a new you with special business superpowers, or with more confidence than you feel, or more money, or friends in higher places. You.

What happens for the rest of this story is up to you.

Take small steps. They will become something big.

Dream. Until your dreams burn white hot.

Push on. Especially when things get hard.

Stay free. For as long as you can.

Give. At least as much as you take.

And – above all – DO IT NOW!

We are all inventors, each sailing out on a voyage of discovery, guided each by a private chart, of which there is no duplicate. The world is all gates, all opportunities, strings of tension waiting to be struck.

Ralph Waldo Emerson

The Creator's
Black Book

THE BEST COLLECTION OF RESOURCES FOR CREATORS THAT WE HAVE EVER SEEN

There is an extraordinary range of help available to you as you work on your idea – and much of it is free. Online and offline, such tools, resources and information are seriously powerful to you as a creator. It's as if the world wants you to do this. Take advantage!

From training to customer surveys, from website building programs to advice and resources about how to get investment, this is our attempt to bring it all together – the good stuff. It's the list of resources and tools that we would have loved to have had when we started out. So here it is in its first ever incarnation: The Creator's Black Book.

Everything in The Creator's Black Book has been used by us or at least recommended to us by someone we trust. They are all seriously valuable resources in their own right – and together they also give you a picture of the ecosystem of technology, assistance and information in which your idea will thrive.

Updates to The Creator's Black Book will be available at the Creator Community on our website, theideainyou.com. We wanted to include a printed version here, though, so that you can start to make use of it immediately. Please do get in touch with us via our website if you know of something we haven't included that you believe will be valuable to other creators. We will add it to our ever-growing online list and to future editions of the book. Please also let us know of any broken links.

To help you navigate it, The Creator's Black Book is grouped into eight sections:

◎ 1. Learning new skills

A list of online and in-person training to help you fill gaps in your skills. So in the early days, you can do as much as possible for your idea yourself – giving you experience and saving you money.

◎ 2. Building your idea

Support for making your idea real. This section includes resources to help you build a website or a blog and even an app, and for commissioning advanced product prototypes if you need them. Whether you want to do this all yourself or hire someone else to do it, this is the definitive list of tools and resources to help make your idea into something real.

◎ 3. Discovery – about your idea, your customers and your market

Researching your market and customer is more fun than it sounds. These days there is a wide range of seriously inspiring ways to help you learn what people and companies think and do, and predict what will make your idea a success. From surveys to clever online tools, we share a set of resources that are instant, global and fun to use.

◎ 4. Building fans

Your idea needs fans. In this section, we share the resources you can use to find users for your idea and build good relationships with them. From email campaigns and social media marketing to online advertising, this is a collection of the most powerful fan-finding resources.

5. Making sales

If you want your idea to become a business, it will have to sell stuff. These days you don't need a shop on the high street – you don't even need a website. The resources we share in this section will help you sell to a global audience, with or without a website of your own. Learn how to create a listing, take payment and dispatch your product around the world.

 ## 6. Getting help

As your idea grows, you may find you need people to help you. In this section we show you how to find the good ones. From sourcing suppliers through to recruiting and collaborating with your first employees, this is how your team will become a happy gang of like-minded individuals.

 ## 7. Finding investment

Once you know how your idea works and makes money, you may decide you want to expand more aggressively, and that you're happy to share in the upside with a partner. We show how getting investment usually works and how you can find the right people to back you and your idea.

 ## 8. Boring but important

To avoid growing pains, we share the vital tools and support services that will stop the boring stuff from getting on top of you. Find out how to get contracts made, accounts kept, and billing and invoicing done on time and without breaking the bank.

1. LEARNING NEW SKILLS

We put this section first, because learning is central to the life of the creator. In the early days especially – while money is tight and you're exploring how powerful your idea can become – it's sensible to learn to do as much as you can yourself. From making a website, to editing a video or designing a logo, or creating a 3D prototype, learning how to do it yourself will save you money and it will give you the invaluable experience of seeing how it's done first-hand.

There is a growing list of high-quality online learning services that provide training for practically every skill a creator might want to learn. Here are our favourites:

www.lynda.com

What is it?
Online video courses for a vast array of technology, creative and business skills, from hand drawing to bookkeeping. The video courses are delivered by experts and cater for all levels of ability.

What's free?
All the courses offer free tutorials so that you can get a feel for the subject and get started. But if you want to access the full series then you will need to become a member – the basic package costs £14.95 a month but you can opt for a ten-day free trial that gives you full access to all content.

top tip
Video training courses like Lynda and Udemy are great for flexible on-the-go learning and they allow you to practise the skill you are mastering in real time as you learn. For more fiddly skills like using software packages this is a massive advantage as it lets you immediately practise what you've been taught.

www.udemy.com

What is it?
Udemy is similar to Lynda in that it offers high-quality online video courses on a wide range of skills, but it is a marketplace where anyone can upload a training course. There is a great selection of courses on design, software and coding in particular.

What's free?
Unlike Lynda, on Udemy there is no subscription. Many courses are offered free by trainers to build their reputation or to link to their product or website. Others charge a one-off fee for lifetime membership of their course – these can range from a few pounds to a few hundred pounds.

www.alison.com

What is it?
Free online training at certificate and diploma level for a good range of business skills that are useful for business beginners or creators.

What's free?
The courses are free and you can study at your own pace. If you are prepared to put the work in this is an amazing free resource for new creators.

> **top tip**
> Before enrolling on a paid course use the free videos on YouTube to get a feel for the topic area and whether it will give you the skills you need.

Learning about business

There are also excellent offline courses, seminars and workshops that train in the wider area of start-up creation:

www.smallbusinesscentre.org.uk

What is it?

The London Small Business Centre is a not-for-profit support agency for small businesses. It offers a range of excellent free services, from access to funding through to weekly three-hour start-up workshops. Some courses cover the basics of getting your idea up and running. Others are more in-depth business training courses which go deeper on the core business skills you will need as your idea grows.

What's free?

The courses are free but, as demand is high, your needs and suitability are assessed prior to acceptance.

www.hyperisland.com

What is it?

Best-in-class training on digital and media topics, such as 'Digital Acceleration'. These are based all around the world as well as major cities in the UK.

What's free?

They are paid-for courses that are not cheap, but you are paying for an immersive experience which will transform how you think about digital business.

Learning how to code

Learn to code! It's easier than it sounds – and is a genuinely transformative experience because it will give you control of your idea on the internet. The best courses cost money, naturally, but are generally worth it. Your relationship with the internet will change, in just a day in many cases.

There are a number of training companies specializing in teaching people how to make simple websites. The one we know to recommend is Decoded's Code_in a Day course – details can be found at **www.decoded.com**.

2. BUILDING YOUR IDEA

As you develop versions of your idea, you will draw on different resources. We advise that you start with the tools you need to bring your idea to life in a simple way (i.e. make your Version Zero) and move on to more sophisticated product prototyping and web developing skills as your idea takes off.

Making early versions of your idea

PowerPoint or Keynote

What are they?
Presentation software for PCs and Macs.

What's free?
If you have a Mac, Keynote will most likely be part of your core software package. PowerPoint is part of Microsoft Office.

> **top tip**
> These are surprisingly good for quickly showing what you mean by your idea, or demoing a website or app (also fully navigable using a touchscreen laptop). Keynote on the Mac gets you a slicker finish in our view.

www.storyboardthat.com

What is it?
A simple piece of software for building a storyboard of your idea.

What's free?
There is a free trial and thereafter you will need to pay a small monthly subscription.

iMovie or Pinnacle studio

What are they?
Easy to use but powerful apps for editing videos on your
smartphone – iMovie for iPhones and iPads and Pinnacle Studios
for Android and iPhone.

What's free?
You will need to pay £2.99 for iMovie and £8.99 for Pinnacle Stu-
dio but it is a one-off cost – and well worth it.

www.withoomph.com

What is it?
An online service that automatically designs high-quality ready-
made logos based on keywords you put in. A fancy logo is a great
way of making your early idea look like a real thing.

What's free?
You have to pay $25 per logo.

Using household products

Why not use Sugru, paper or card to make a Version Zero of your idea. Here are a couple of YouTube videos for inspiration:

Getting creative with Sugru: **https://www.youtube.com/watch?v=DXtbNqJzwjA**

Making paper and household product prototypes: **https://youtube.com/watch?v=tqycVQGw1-M**

Making a website

There is a huge range of excellent and quite easy-to-use online packages designed to help you build a website yourself. If your site is just for providing people with some information about your idea – i.e. it doesn't need to take payment, or have log-in functionality – a simple publishing platform like this will do the job brilliantly:

WordPress (https://wordpress.org) is an excellent place to start. Most smaller websites built by creators (and many with lots of traffic) are built on the WordPress platform, including theideainyou.com. There's a fairly steep learning curve at the beginning as you discover how websites work, but it's worth sticking with it. It's easier than it looks and once you have the basics, you will be able to design and update your website yourself, which will make your life a lot easier in the long run, since you won't have to pay/ask someone else to do it.

There is a wide range of 'templates' which offer a slick and well-built 'off the shelf' format for your site. You just insert your content into a style of your choosing. Here are a few that we have enjoyed using:

themeforest.net

If it is a template you are after – especially for a WordPress site – then it will be here! This is a marketplace of nearly 20,000 templates to choose from. Take your time to look at the demos – you will almost certainly be able to find a website theme that works for your idea's needs and style.

elegantthemes.com

Another source of well-made themes. Elegant Themes design and support a wide range of themes. Their offer is particularly good for you if you like to change your site regularly since they sell their entire range of sites for a fixed fee (eighty-seven themes for $69 at the time of writing).

Domain names, hosting and analytics

Whatever site you are building, you will need a domain name (like theideainyou.com). You will then need somewhere to host it (this is where your site lives on the internet, essentially a server somewhere).

We bought the URL for theideainyou.com from godaddy.com and chose to host it on gandi.net. There are other companies that do the same thing. The system for setting up is pretty straightforward and the support systems they offer are designed to help someone with very little experience get their website up.

https://uk.godaddy.com

What is it?
Godaddy will sell you the domain name for your site if it's available (the central register of names is sold by a range of intermediaries of which Godaddy is one) and they will offer you hosting for your site (i.e. where all the code sits on the internet) with the features you need. Reliable service and great support make Godaddy very popular among creators we spoke to.

What's free?
It is free to search the availability of website URLs but you will need to pay to own and host them.

> **top tip**
> The price of a domain name will be dependent on the name you want to register (assuming it is available). Get an

entry-level hosting package. Until you get lots of traffic (i.e. many thousands of visitors a day), this will be enough.

gandi.net; www.linode.com; www.hostgator.com

What are they?
Reliable, powerful and good value hosting services where you can register your domain and host your website, as well as store and aggregate your business's data (emails, documents, etc.).

What's free?
These are paid-for services but they offer great value for money and reliable service.

top tip
They offer excellent and free 24/7 customer service – many offer a 'live chat' function where you can get help from a support person. They expect you to lean on their expertise to get your hosting set up, and to solve any teething troubles, so make the most of it.

Stock photography

Putting good photography on your website will help your site look professional from day one, and can make your idea look good. The legal bottom line is that you can't use other people's photos unless you have an agreement with them. You must use your own shots, pay for stock photography or find a source of free royalty-free images.

For stock photography, try **www.istockphoto.com** or **www. shutterstock.com**. Both offer discount packages on a huge range of images. From any of stock photography platform, you can download a free low-res version of an image (i.e. it will be slightly blurry and may have a watermark on it) and try it on your site to see if you like it before you buy the hi-res image.

For more cost-effective options check out **https://500px. com** and **www.flickr.com/creativecommons**.

There are also free stock images and videos here:

bootstrapbay.com/blog/free-stock-photos/
https://medium.com/@dustin/stock-photos-that-dont-suck-62ae4bcbe01b
www.sitebuilderreport.com/stock-up
www.pexels.com
allthefreestock.com

You can also take your own pictures, of course. Most smartphones have good enough lenses and processors to shoot hi-res images these days. There is also a fast-expanding range of photo editing apps for both iPhone and Android that will help you make your pictures look crisp and interesting. Have a look for reviews of these online, or visit the App Store.

Making physical prototypes

If your idea is a physical product then you may decide to pay to have a high-quality 3D prototype made. Here are a few services that will help you make a good prototype cost effectively:

www.ponoko.com

What is it?
An online prototyping service that makes great value prototypes of 3D products, using a range of methods from handmade craft to 3D printing.

What's free?
You get a free digital (i.e. 2D) prototype of your product before you commit to buying.

top tip
Check what your finished prototype will look like before you commit. This service is well worth using, to help you get a sense of what you will be paying for and to improve it before you hit 'make'.

www.makerscafe.com

What is it?

A collection of 3D printing cafés in the US and Europe. There is a London branch in Shoreditch. It offers a space for creators to meet, get free consultancy and paid-for training as well as have their 3D prototypes printed live in-store.

What's free?

The consultancy service is free but you will need to pay to have CAD wireframes of your product made and for it to be 3D printed.

top tip

Have a coffee and chat to the team and other creators. They offer a free consultancy service, so spend time chatting through your project before getting your wireframes made.

Finally, when you come to make market-ready prototypes of your product, you might want to check out a trade show in your industry, so you can meet suppliers in person. Do a Google search to find these.

You can also head straight to sites such as **www.thomasnet.com** and **www.alibaba.com** which collate expert manufacturers of every product imaginable and connect you directly with them.

It's worth taking the time to find a trusted manufacturer. Quality is mostly very high, but it's wise to ask for references and to talk to a previous client if you can, just to learn more about your supplier before you commit to spending money with them. If orders arrive late or incomplete or are not built to spec, it can be a difficult drain on your time and resources.

Hiring a designer

In the early days of your idea's development, learning to do as much of your design as you can yourself can really help keep costs down. The rudiments of packages like InDesign and Photoshop can be learned quite quickly and easily with online training and through home practice. If you need expert design, though, perhaps to help you create a more professional logo, pack design or website, it has never been easier to access expertise.

There are many thousands of excellent designers out there, who work remotely and are ready to help you. There is also an interesting range of ways to employ them. From crowd-sourcing to sites which help you find specialists to work hourly on your project, the choices are plentiful and growing.

Before you dive in, here are a couple of tips to help oil the wheels:

top tip 1

Design is nuanced and subjective, so briefing it requires impeccable communication. To get the best out of a remote designer, you have to know what you want and be able to communicate it clearly to them. Before you start briefing a designer, make sure that you can explain clearly what you want and what you don't want. Try briefing a friend to see how they interpret your instructions. A designer won't be able to solve fundamental confusions you have about your idea, but they should be able to bring your vision to life beautifully if you can explain clearly what you have in mind.

top tip 2

Explore what you want. Draw pictures. Be as visual as you can. Use examples you like from other brands, products, designs, websites and magazines. The more you can bring your brief to life visually, the easier it will be for your designers to nail it first time and with minimum cost.

Crowd-sourcing design work

Crowd-sourcing means putting your brief in front of a wide range of experts so that they can bid for the work. Essentially, a pool of designers will be able to look at your brief and how much you are prepared to pay, and decide whether they would like to pitch for your job.

Crowd-sourcing websites put the following creative skills at your service:

- Logo design
- Company naming
- Graphic design
- Web page and app screen design
- Product imagery
- Product packaging
- Idea generation
- Animation
- Illustration
- Storyboards
- Magazine and book layouts
- Copy writing
- Blog post writing

The process involved in crowd-sourcing design services depends on the type of job you are briefing and the system the website you are using believes works best. Generally, every site is trying to make the process as fair as possible to both parties, and as good as possible at creating excellent work.

With small jobs, like getting a logo made, it is usually as simple as this: you upload your brief and say what you are willing to pay. Designers then submit their response to your brief and you select the submission that you like the best, and pay for it. Often, the designers will actually do the work as part of their pitch (designing a logo or writing some copy, for example), so you get to see a range of solutions to your brief and pick the one you want to pay for.

For larger jobs, you generally have to select from *proposals* given by designers in response to your brief. Usually, these include examples of past work, detail on how they plan to approach your project, and their costs and timings.

Prices and quality vary, because anyone can respond to your brief. Work out what you can have for free, be as clear as you can and commit only when you see something you are excited by. We recommend trying the full range of sites and putting your brief on all of them. Listing is generally free. Most sites offer a money-back guarantee too – and whatever happens, you only pay once you are happy with the work. Above all, be fair and treat others as you would like to be treated.

99designs.co.uk

One of the best services out there due to the broad range of design and creative work on offer – and the quality of the designers waiting to have a crack at your brief. Make this your first port of call.

www.crowdspring.com

The world's number 1 marketplace for logos, graphic design and naming.

A great resource for both crowd-sourcing smaller jobs as well as hooking up with specialist designers for bigger jobs.

www.conceptcupboard.com

There is a smaller selection of designers to choose from on here, but the results can still be powerful and prices are competitive.

Finding design freelancers

These next sites are marketplaces for freelancers. You can browse them and find someone whose work you like and hire them by the day and for extended periods. For a bigger job you might want to hire a freelancer for an extended period, so that you can use them flexibly over time on a series of tasks. They'll spend more time on your project, so it's worth finding someone you trust.

www.upwork.com

A great range of quality freelancers available for small, large and team projects. The project-tracking functionality also makes it easy for you to manage your project.

www.peopleperhour.com

A site that hooks recruiters up with a wide range of skilled free-lancers. Here you can get copy written for a leaflet, wireframes made for your app, even a press release written.

A note on making apps . . .

If your idea is to build an app, then we'd like to dispel a couple of myths.

The first is that apps are cheap. Good apps cost proper money. They require significant front-end (user experience and design) work and back-end (the engine that drives the performance of your app) development work.

The second myth is that you build just one app and then watch the money roll in. In fact, you have to build the same one several times over. To keep your app up to date, improving and working on the latest handsets and operating systems, you will need to offer new releases regularly. You will require one of these at least every twelve months. These usually necessitate sizeable front- and back-end investment.

There are also hosting fees and licence costs – which can easily come to £150 a month.

Before you commit to making an app, work out whether you actually need one. Websites are much cheaper to build and maintain and can be a good place to start and learn about your idea before you invest in making an app. We find **howmuchtomakeanapp. com/estimator** a useful resource, in particular its 'App Vs. Web-site' page. This will help you get a ballpark understanding of how much your app will cost to make.

If we haven't put you off already, and you remain convinced that an app is the right medium for your idea, here are our five golden rules:

* *Do some learning first*: **www.thechocolatelabapps.com**, **www.udemy.com** and **www.lynda.com** are great sources of advice and training for beginners.

- *Do a lot of sketching before you start building*: Make sure you are clear on the concept for your app and you know how people will use it and benefit from it. Taking time and care to get the functionality and user experience right is critical to making a great app.
- *Partner smartly; get good people*: Find the right mix of UX (the design of the User Experience, i.e. the flow and look of the app) and back-end development (the foundation, engine and brain of the app which makes sure it runs smoothly and intelligently) for your idea. Pick the wrong team and your costs will spiral.
- *Start with iPhone*: iPhone apps are generally easier, faster and much cheaper to build than Android apps. Get your app right on Apple's iOS software before you invest in building an Android version.
- *Do your wireframes yourself*: Wireframes are simple sketches that show how users will navigate your app. Even if you are going to outsource all of your app's development, designing how your app works – its wireframes – will mean you have to get really clear on the experience you want to give your users. This will save you time and money in development. Mockingbird (**https://gomockingbird.com**) and POP (**https://popapp.in**) are great tools to help you do this.

3. DISCOVERY – ABOUT YOUR IDEA, YOUR CUSTOMERS AND YOUR MARKET

As you bring your idea to fruition, what you focus on will depend on your instincts, and the information you can get from the world. If you can build a picture of what is happening out there – around your idea, your users and your market – then you can make a powerful plan for how you are going to grow. Information is power.

We take the view that the best combination is an open mind fed with inspiring information. Here are the tools that have inspired action in us with the minimum of fuss and complexity:

www.surveymonkey.com

What is it?
An easy-to-use system for sending out a quick survey to your customer base. Surveys are useful to get quick learning from a wide group of people or to get proactive customer feedback on your product or service.

What's free?
Sending a survey is free but if you want to run more sophisticated analytics or read more than a hundred responses you will have to pay a small fee.

> **top tip**
> You can use surveys as a sales tactic. Ask people what they want you to add to your idea, build it in, and then let them know that you've done it. For more on this, and much else, check out Jeff Walker's quite brilliant Product Launch Formula at **productlaunchformula.com**.

www.trackur.com

What is it?
A social media monitoring tool that lets you see what's being discussed on the main social media platforms. You can search by brands, keywords and trends.

What's free?
Trackur offer a free ten-day trial with no commitment to buy the service afterwards.

top tip
It's energizing to see when your idea is being mentioned but social media monitoring is also helpful to show you what else people are talking about. This can be useful if your idea sits in a trend-driven marketplace like restaurants, fashion, music or film.

https://adwords.google.com/KeywordPlanner

What is it?
A quick and extremely powerful way to find out what people are searching for online and in what numbers. Just type in the keywords you're interested in (e.g. 'vegan restaurant') and see how many searches that term is getting (answer now: around 3 million a month!). You can also explore what more specific searches are being made (e.g. 'NYC vegan restaurant' at 9,300 per month) so you can see what sections of the market are particularly sought after.

What's free?
The service is free but you need a Gmail account.

top tip
Get a sense of what people are searching for around your idea – it will help you understand what they care about. **www.google.com/insights** also lets you see how many people have been searching for a certain phrase in the last decade. Try searching for trends over time related to specific searches. 'Vegan restaurant' is at its highest ever since Google

records began back in 2004. Google Trends also shows
regional data (top city for searches of 'vegan restaurant':
Los Angeles).

Analytics

Most analytics measure online activity. If you connect analytics to your site, every customer interaction with your website or online advertising or marketing can be tracked and logged. This gives you access to invaluable information about what is working, and it gives you the thrill of understanding who is reading, buying or sharing your idea.

You can see how people found your website, which parts of the website people spend most time on, when they visited, what they clicked on. Without analytics you are essentially in the dark about how your online activity is performing. With even the simplest understanding of it, you have priceless real-time information at your fingertips which will help you make your online presence work even harder for you.

To have all this all you have to do is put a small amount of code onto your site, which Google will give you for free (and they'll show you what to do with it), and then you can dive into analytics.

www.google.com/analytics

What is it?
A free service from Google showing detailed statistics about your website's traffic.

What's free?
The basic analytics service is free and works well for most sites.

top tip
If you have a website, connect it to Google Analytics. This is the brain behind your online activity. Take the time to make sure that all your online activity is plugged into it so you can see where people come from and what they do on your site.

There are other excellent analytics products, such as **https://mixpanel.com** and **www.geckoboard.com**. These offer more sophisticated analytics on simple and intuitive dashboards for accessing your data in real time. We recommend you start with Google Analytics and branch out to these if you want more firepower.

Learning about your market

The best way to learn about how your market works is to find people who know about it and connect with them.

www.meetup.com

What is it?
A free online network which puts you in touch with people in your local area who share the same interests as you do.

What's free?
It is free to set up an account but you have to pay 'organizer's dues' to set up and lead Meetup groups. These are nominal sums and if you are unhappy with the service you can request a refund inside the first thirty days of membership.

top tip
Meetups are a good way to connect quickly with people who are already working in your sector, but it can also help you reach potential consumers if you want to test your idea with them.

https://www.linkedin.com/premium/products

What is it?
The world's largest business social network. Your target audience, your competitors and industry experts are all on here for you to connect with them.

What's free?
You will need to have a LinkedIn profile (which is free) and you

can then run a free month-long trial of Premium that will let you send fifteen free messages directly to other creators and experts.

The British Library/Business & IP Centre

What is it?
The British Library in London is the national library of the UK, holding over 170 million books – the most comprehensive collection of business books and materials in the UK. The business content is divided into four categories – market research, company information, trade directories and journals – and is housed in the Business & IP Centre. This centre also offers free expert advice, consultation and support on a range of topics. You can discuss your initial idea with an expert and get advice on how to protect your intellectual property and apply for a patent.

What's free?
Many of the services are free. Some you will be asked to pay a small fee for.

www.facebook.com/advertising

What is it?
A tool that lets you plan Facebook advertising campaigns – and in

the process you can learn about the interests, demographics and location of your target audience.

What's free?
The process of planning and targeting your advert is free and that is how you will find out about your audience. If you go on to actually post the ad, there is a fee.

top tip
If you are planning where to put a store, pop-up or retail concession, Facebook ads is a quick way of seeing where your target market is clustered geographically. It can also be useful in deciding where to focus offline marketing, distribution and stockists.

www.twazzup.com

What is it?
A Twitter search engine. This is a great tool for finding out who the influencers in your sector are, and what they're talking about. It's also great for tracking who is talking about your idea.

What's free?
The basic tools are free and are more than enough if you are just using this as a tool to research your market.

top tip
If you need to find a niche specialist to help you with your idea this can be a great platform to identify influencers and experts.

www.duedil.com

What is it?
A slick interface that allows you to quickly and easily search Companies House for industry and competitor information and financial performance data. You can also use this to see how competitive your marketplace is, or to find companies to collaborate with.

What's free?

The basic search is free but advanced searching functionality, which you will need if you want to use the market-sizing functionality, will require you to sign up to a monthly contract (starting at £24.99 a month).

top tip 1

If your idea is something that you will sell directly to businesses then the market-sizing tool is a really handy way of seeing where the kinds of businesses you'd want to work with or sell to are located and how many of them there are.

top tip 2

DueDil is also handy for checking out suppliers before you commit to spending money with them. It will flag credit health and potential risks.

4. BUILDING FANS

As you refine and build your idea, you will want to grow your fan base and start to generate revenue. This can be a heady period as you invest time and sometimes cash growing the reach of your idea. It's exciting, though, because you see your tribes swelling.

Thanks to the internet there is a range of tools and techniques nowadays which allow you to communicate with large numbers of people. To help you understand your choices, we have focused on the main online tools that will help you generate the best results for minimum investment.

Email marketing

Email is a powerful medium. One of these landing in your inbox means more than a Facebook post or a tweet, because it's got your name on it. Email is a great medium for communicating regularly with your customers, keeping them up to date on what you have to offer them. You might send a regular newsletter, or tactical commercial messages like special offers. There are lots of providers out there, many offering a very similar service. Here are two that we trust:

mailchimp.com

What is it?
Our preferred email marketing software. A tried and trusted service that is great for beginners.

What's free?
The 'Entrepreneur' package lets you mail up to 2,000 subscribers and is free as long as you stay within the limit. Note – costs go up fast once your list grows beyond that point.

www.yesware.com

What is it?
Another great piece of email marketing software. Its one big
advantage over MailChimp is that it integrates directly into Gmail
and Outlook, meaning that you can plan, send and track campaign emails from your regular email account in real time, without
having to log in to a separate piece of software.

What's free?
It is free to trial on your personal emails – up to 100 a month and
the next package up, 'Pro', is reasonably priced, at $12 a month.

Writing better emails

Great sales emails and newsletters need a bit of copywriting know-
how. Even a good subject line will increase the number of people
who will open your email. Before you hit send, take the time to do
some learning online about what works best. As always, YouTube
is a good place to start learning about how to use the internet.
Here are two videos to get you started:

Subject lines that will increase your open rates and your click-
through rates:
https://www.youtube.com/watch?v=X3-jvu5YaiA
How to create an email newsletter that doesn't suck:
https://www.youtube.com/watch?v=mGSPj4CyOMQ

Capturing emails – with squeeze pages and sign-ups

One of the most valuable resources as your idea grows is your list of prospects. This is the list of people who have shown any interest in your idea, and – crucially, since this is how you will communicate with them – their email addresses.

Whatever you do, make sure that you build email capturing into your processes. So long as you have their agreement, you can start communicating with people directly after you have their email address. If you capture emails from visitors to your site, you can send them newsletters, special content to build their trust in you, and offers.

To get their email address, you might offer them a free trial, or a free gift that they would value, or some money off your product. Capturing an email on your site is now very easy. You simply place a pre-made template (a 'plug-in') on your site which gives the visitor a couple of lines where they can write their details. This is then sent to your email marketing software and triggers an automatic email message saying hello and giving them the opportunity to 'opt-in' (i.e. agree to be on your list). Once they're in you can follow up with further communication. People can unsubscribe, or divert your emails to their spam inbox at any time, so it is essential to offer value consistently.

www.getdrip.com

What is it?
A great-looking widget that you can plug in to your site to let users sign up for newsletters or competitions.

What's free?
You can get a free three-week trial – after that you need to pay a monthly subscription.

www.megaphoneapp.com

What is it?
An excellent range of page templates – squeeze pages, buy pages,
download pages – which are ready to go. Use these to turn someone on your site into a prospect – capture their email, sell them an
e-book, get them to register for an event.

What's free?
You can try out the pages for free, but as soon as you want to put
them live on the internet, you have to pay.

Social media marketing

Social media is a powerful way to spread the word about your idea
and build fans. It can also be a bit of a black hole for your time, so
we advise that you follow these three basic steps:

1. Pick the right platform for your idea

There are six mainstream social media platforms – Facebook, Instagram, Twitter, Google+, Pinterest and LinkedIn.

Each of these will include most segments of society, but some
are most popular with certain audiences. Facebook and Instagram,
for example, are very popular with mums and LinkedIn with professionals and businesses. Google+ is good for reaching a more

male audience which is interested in technology. Twitter is used by many journalists, fashionistas, politicos and film buffs.

Creating fans on social media takes time, effort and commitment. We suggest focusing on one ideal platform first – the right one for your needs. Spend time researching the different platforms, by searching using keywords related to your idea until you can see which ones will reach your target audience best.

Consider also which platform offers the best media for your idea. For example Instagram and Pinterest are very visual. Facebook and Twitter are better for interaction and announcements. If your idea is a home-decoration business then Pinterest might work well. If it is a restaurant, then Twitter will allow you to share news about your menu and special offers with diners. If it is a campaign, Facebook may work best. Find brands you respect in your market and see what they are doing on social media.

2. Build fans, don't buy them

There is a range of dubious paid-for services that promise you followers, fans and likes in exchange for payment. Avoid them. You need real fans, not pretend ones. It is far more important to have energy in your online community than pure numbers.

To build a community of fans you will need to invest time and love. Be nice, be honest and share content, discounts and added value with them. Over time, you will build a relationship valued by both parties.

3. Learn the skills

There are a number of high-quality training courses online that will teach you how to swell your numbers and make your social media activity really effective. **www.udemy.com** and **www.lynda.com** both offer a wide range of free basic courses and some you have to pay for. Read reviews to see which course will be most valuable for you.

There are also established experts on specific platforms, such as Martin Shervington **www.martinshervington.com** on Google+ and Hilary Rushford on Instagram (**@HilaryRushford**). These people know what they are doing and will help you learn. You can usually sign up to their free newsletter, offering great tips and often training before you commit to any paid courses.

We also recommend that you spend time looking at how other people and brands you admire use social media. Go to their website, and follow links to their most popular social media feeds. Take a look at their activity. What content are they sharing? How are they building their following?

Tracking social media

There are some excellent free resources that will help you keep an eye on what is happening on social media. You can plan your own social media activity, and see who else is talking about your idea or your market. Here are three of our favourites:

https://about.twitter.com/products/tweetdeck

An excellent tool. The simplest way to plan and track your twitter activity.

www.iconosquare.com

Track hashtag mentions on Instagram – of your idea or anything else you want to know about.

www.tweetreach.com

See where your tweets go. Find your most influential followers and work out who to target to get the maximum reach.

Online advertising

If you have an online presence, online advertising is one of the fastest ways to get people to visit it. Essentially you 'buy' audience from the biggest websites by placing ads with them which connect to your website.

At the moment, there are four dominant online advertising platforms: Google, Facebook, LinkedIn and Twitter. Each of these uses a 'Pay Per Click' (PPC) model. This means they put your ad on their platform and you pay a small fee every time someone clicks on it. You decide where the person who clicks on your ad is sent to – usually a page on your site where they can buy something so that you get the cost of the click back and more.

If you've got something you can sell to them, and you can convert a good proportion of people who arrive on that page, this kind of advertising is a great tool. Costs depend on the platform and how many other advertisers are competing for the same clicks, but tend to range from a few pence to several pounds. The good thing about Pay Per Click advertising is that you pay only when someone clicks – and you can set the amount you want to pay per click and the budget you are happy to spend each day.

There are three things for you to focus on:

Picking the right channel – deciding which of the four platforms to focus your activity on, based on where you think your customers are.

Deciding on your targeting – planning which 'keywords' you want to trigger your ad (e.g. the words that a user has to type into Google to make your ad appear, or the interests listed by the Facebook users you want to see your ad) – so that it generates as much quality traffic as possible.

Writing your message – you are looking for a compelling message that makes only the right people click through. Remember you pay for every click – so it's worth making sure that the message puts off the people you don't want as much as brings in the customers you do.

1. Picking your channel

For many campaigns, a combination of the main platforms will reach a significant chunk of your potential customer universe. So, the wise advice would be to start small on two or three of them, and test what's working. Try things on a small scale, so you can learn and refine your approach. For some campaigns, just one of the big four will stand out as the obvious platform. For instance, if your idea targets small business owners then LinkedIn would be a smart place to start.

2. Smartly targeting your ad

If you get your pay-per-click keywords right, your ad will drive the right people to your website at the lowest possible price.

In the world of online advertising, different words give you different reach and come with different costs. Some keywords are seriously expensive because they are so competitive. When someone types the words 'car insurance' or 'engagement ring' into Google, advertisers know that they can make hundreds or even thousands of pounds from that customer. Google knows that the value of the customer is high, so they will charge top dollar for those keywords. In fact, it's an auction, where the price is automatically based on how much advertisers are bidding for those clicks, and how many advertisers there are in the market for them. Our advice is to set your budget low, and to do some experiments. Learn which words bring you the greatest return for the lowest cost.

Before you start, watch a few online tutorials on YouTube. This one from Google is particularly good: **https://www.youtube.com/watch?v=zUMQCn6KWzA**

3. Getting your messaging right

Online advertising is not the same as 'brand advertising' – where you tell stories about your product to give it meaning for people. This is 'direct response' advertising. Here you are triggering an immediate action from your target audience (i.e. clicking through to your site or a landing page).

The big four platforms offer basic tutorials about the messages that get the best response. But if you are going to be doing a lot of online advertising, the best investment you can make is to take the time to read one (or both) of these books:

Ogilvy on Advertising

Written by the advertising giant of the last century, David Ogilvy, founder of the Ogilvy advertising empire. It is a brutally simple and excellently written exposé on how advertising messages work and how to write them.

How to Write a Good Advertisement

This book by Victor O. Schwab offers an excellent 'how-to' guide for writing advertising copy that gets results.

top tip

Put a cap on the budget you are willing to spend to keep costs under control. Start small and experiment before you put significant budget behind any message. Write a few different advertising messages and post all of them at the same time. All platforms offer you the means to do this so you can see which is most effective. Spot those that give the best return on your investment, and repeat them.

Creating landing pages

To get the very best conversion rates from online advertising it helps to have a bespoke landing page that your ad clicks through to. The purpose of this is to close the deal, that is, let visitors complete the action your ad is offering – buy your product, access some special content or sign up to something – all without having to hunt around your site.

unbounce.com

What is it?
A service that helps you create mobile and web landing pages – no IT expertise needed.

What's free?
They offer a thirty-day free trial with no commitment to buy afterwards.

top tip
It can take time to create a good landing page but the rewards in conversion will be worth it. Take your time and use Unbounce's freephone customer service if you need it.

www.leadpages.net

What is it?
LeadPages offers one of the easiest to use and most intuitive services for building landing pages.

What's free?
You will need to pay a monthly subscription but they offer a thirty-day money-back guarantee if you are not satisfied with the service.

top tip
Their range of great landing-page templates helps you quickly and easily customize your campaign rather than build from scratch. Try out a range of different landing pages to help you refine what you're trying to do – then pick your favourite.

Managing campaigns

When you are advertising regularly online, it helps to be able to manage all your online campaigns across a range of platforms on one single dashboard. It makes it quicker and easier to plan, launch and track your activity. We recommend giving AdStage a trial.

www.adstage.io

What is it?
An all-in-one advertising platform that lets you seamlessly manage Google, Facebook, Twitter, LinkedIn and Bing ads.

What's free?
AdStage offer a no-strings-attached fourteen-day free trial but then costs $99 a month.

top tip

The 'Campaign Creation' tool is a brilliant resource that gives bespoke advice on the best way to set up your ads for each platform you are advertising on.

5. MAKING SALES

Selling your idea through a marketplace

You don't even need your own website to sell things online. There is a range of marketplaces, all of which will sell your product for you. All you need to do is have a product and list it with them.

Amazon and eBay are the originals in this category. Both offer comprehensive guides and tutorials on how to set up as a vendor and start selling today.

With eBay, you will need to fulfil your product yourself (i.e. send it out to the buyer). Amazon will fulfil your product for you if you want them to. Just create a product listing and send your product in bulk to their warehouse.

You may also choose to fulfil your Amazon sales yourself. This gives you access to more customer data, but means you need a system in place for delivering the product to buyers promptly 365 days of the year and for dealing with returns.

There are other smaller specialist marketplaces that allow you to sell your product or content. Such providers will charge commission on sales made through their site, and some charge set-up fees too.

www.etsy.com

Anyone can create a shop on this craft marketplace. Focused on unique, unusual and handmade or vintage items (not mass-market or mainstream products or brands).

www.notonthehighstreet.com

For niche products that aren't produced in the volume needed in mainstream chains. You must apply to get your product listed first (instructions are on the site), but we understand they are a good partner and drive a lot of traffic to their site, so a good product can expect good sales.

https://gumroad.com

The best platform for selling digital content (downloads) of all kinds – music, software, e-books, video. Gumroad is not a 'market-place' – i.e. you do not compete with other sellers on there. You just set up your own page and drive your customers to it. Gum-road take a small commission on every sale.

Putting a shop on your website

As your idea grows, you may choose to sell your idea on your own site. Like most things on the internet, creating an online shop is much easier than it used to be.

A range of templates exist that are designed to help you put a professional-looking shop on your website. All offer a free demo. This means you can work out if the features they offer are the right ones for selling your product. We recommend that you do a dry run yourself, installing the pages and 'buying' your own product so that you can experience the process as both buyer and seller and check that it works.

https://tictail.com

A brilliant free-to-use platform that lets you create an online store straight away using their template layouts. It is primarily, but not exclusively, used by creative businesses in the fashion and design sectors. While the core functionality is free you will have to pay for enhanced functionality.

www.shopify.com

The granddaddy of e-commerce sites. A wide range of templates makes this the most popular selling platform around.

cart66.com

Cart66 is built to connect well with WordPress. It's one of the few e-commerce plug-ins that offers a free basic service that is well-suited to a simple experience and low transaction volumes – great for when you are starting out.

Taking payment

If you don't want to build e-commerce functionality into your site, there are options using external payment systems. Essentially you borrow the transaction services from another site by putting their 'buy' button on yours. The payment is taken by someone else and forwarded to you.

www.paypal.com

What is it?
The most familiar of payment processors. PayPal is trusted by many buyers – and it's easy to put a 'buy' button on your site, which then forwards the transaction to PayPal's systems and then on to you.

What's free?
There is a fee on all transactions, though this is reduced if you are a non-profit business.

top tip
PayPal's exchange rates can be pretty poor – almost the same as you get for your holiday money. So if you are selling internationally, consider exchanging your foreign earnings into pounds elsewhere. We understand that **transferwise.com** will support payment from PayPal soon.

www.izettle.com

What is it?
A solution for taking card payments in person. You need a compatible smartphone or tablet – and their card reader gadget.

What's free?

Downloading the app is free and the 'chip and pin lite' terminal is free for limited companies – though if you are a sole trader you will need to pay for it. You pay between 1.5 and 2.75 per cent on each transaction depending on volume.

> **top tip**
> Make the most of the follow-up functionality, which allows you to continue the relationship with customers after they've bought from you.

https://gocardless.com

What is it?

A simple service for taking recurring payments from customers; this is great for subscriptions.

What's free?

It is a paid-for service but a very reasonable one – 1 per cent fee per transaction which is capped at £2. Sign up for the pro service if you plan to be processing high volumes of payments.

> **top tip**
> GoCardless works best for automating regular direct-debit payments for subscriptions.

https://payments.amazon.com

What is it?

Amazon Payments is a simple way for you to take payment on your site without building full e-commerce functionality in the code on your site. Amazon customers use their Amazon login to make the payment for your product, which means they don't need to register or give new details when they buy from you.

What's free?

Amazon Payments promise to refund your transaction fees (there is no sign-up cost) if you haven't seen an increase in sales within thirty days.

Fulfilment

Fulfilment means getting your physical product from the warehouse to the buyer. Most creators do their own fulfilment in the early days. A pile of boxes in their spare room or shed is their warehousing facility and a trip to the post office when they get an order is their fulfilment strategy. We recommend that all creators do this when they start out. You get an understanding of the number of orders an outsourced fulfilment house will need to honour, and you learn what buyers require in terms of after-sales service.

Once the orders are coming in thick and fast, you can consider employing a professional facility to take all this off your hands. There is a range of companies around the world that offer fulfilment services. In the UK we have heard good things about the Fulfilling Station in Bristol (**https://www.thefulfillingsta tion.co.uk**) and James and James (**www.ecommercefulfil ment.com**). If you need international warehousing and fulfilment, take a look at Shipwire (**www.shipwire.com**).

Be aware that storage can be a big cost. If your product takes up lots of room in the warehouse, or takes a while to turn over, fulfilment will get pricey. Before you work with a fulfilment operation, make sure that you have a solid idea about how many items you expect to sell per month and what volume of storage you need in their warehouse. They will offer you a quote. Compare that to doing it yourself.

Managing sales leads

As your marketing activity begins to generate leads and sales, so you start generating data. The identity and contact details of people who are interested in your idea are valuable, because you can convert these people into buyers. Putting the right structures in place for capturing and sorting this data is a sensible move for any creator.

Here are two services that we believe are the most powerful. They offer a range of more sophisticated tools as your idea and needs grow over time. Essentially they keep all your customer information in one place and enable you to communicate appropriately with them, depending on what they have done in the past.

www.salesforce.com

What is it?
A powerful professional platform that helps you organize and track your customers.

What's free?
There is a free thirty-day trial. After that you will need to sign up to a twelve-month contract.

top tip
The mass email functionality is hard to use and doesn't have a particularly impressive range of templates. We'd advise using a separate piece of software, like MailChimp; it syncs easily with Salesforce anyway.

www.infusionsoft.com

What is it?
Infusionsoft is a seriously powerful customer relationship (CRM) platform which lets you automate email campaigns based on what your customers do. This intelligent platform allows you to 'tag' a customer each time they click a link or buy something on your site, and then trigger relevant outbound emails.

What's free?

Infusionsoft is not cheap (around $200 to $300 a month) but it automates much of your marketing and increases your conversion, so if your business is mostly online, your investment will pay back very quickly.

top tip

For complex products like these, there is an extended sales process – take advantage of their excellent sales people and build a picture of how you will use their product before you commit.

6. GETTING HELP

Once your idea takes off you may get very busy, and require help in certain areas. From finding a partner through to working with suppliers and experts, here are the resources we recommend to enable you to access that help easily.

Finding a co-founder

Some people like to travel alone – some like company. If you want company, a co-founder can be one of the best ways to share in the joy and pain of making something wonderful. The best co-founder is arguably someone you already know and trust, but if there's no one suitable available to you right now, you can try these resources:

www.founderdating.com

A networking site where you can meet and hang out in person with well-vetted professionals wanting to join start-ups.

www.cofounderslab.com

Another great resource for meeting up with like-minded professionals looking to join start-ups – a great place to find specialist tech co-founders in particular.

www.workinstartups.com

Offers a pool of highly skilled talent looking to move across to start-ups.

startupweekend.org

A brilliant series of global events that brings new start-ups and professionals together. Over the fifty-four hours new teams are formed and new start-ups launched – look out for one in a city near you.

www.founder2be.com

Another place to meet co-founders, especially tech ones, and specialist team members to help you develop your idea.

Finding suppliers

The best way to find good suppliers is to speak to other creators and find out whom they trust. There are also some aggregating websites that help you speak directly to manufacturers and suppliers abroad:

www.alibaba.com

What is it?
The world's largest business-to-business marketplace, Alibaba connects you with a massive range of predominantly Asian manufacturers and suppliers directly.

What's free?
The merchant pays. It is free to buy through Alibaba, but sellers are charged a fee for your business.

top tip
Be cautious and take your time. Dig for information on the manufacturer and order in very small quantities first to gauge quality before you buy in volume. Keep an eye on minimum order quantities (MOQ) too – most sellers will be happy to negotiate on this.

www.globalsources.com

What is it?
Similar to Alibaba, but focused exclusively on the Chinese market.

What's free?
It is free to sign up. Sellers have to pay membership and advertising fees.

top tip
Make sure you have fully researched a supplier and start with some small test production runs. Keep an eye on shipping costs and import duty too.

www.smartchinasourcing.com, a blog run by Global Sources, is a good source of information on how you can find, verify and work with good Chinese merchants. It is well worth a read before you begin contacting suppliers.

Finding experts

LinkedIn and Google searches are still the best ways to find relevant experts in most fields. You can find the right person for your task and contact them directly. Most people who want to charge for their help have websites. You will find that many people are happy to offer a few words of advice if you contact them directly, even when you don't intend to hire them. As always, be respectful of people's time.

Failing that, there is one specialist marketplace we have found that connects creators with experts in business for small bits of work and advice:

https://clarity.fm

What is it?
Get trusted, market-leading specialist advice on the phone within seventy-two hours for a flat fee.

What's free?
You pay by the minute and costs depend on the expert you want to speak to.

Recruiting

As your idea grows, you may find you need to share the load. It pays to take the time to make sure you get the right person on the right contract. Here are the best resources for finding people, and some which offer guidance on how to work with them.

Interns

Hiring an intern can be a good way to get enthusiastic help in the early days of your idea.

Internship works best when it is mutually beneficial: i.e. when it's a powerful learning experience for the intern and a low-cost and productive labour solution for you. Use an intern on a special project or campaign – it will give them exposure to stimulating and dynamic work and you another pair of hands to help with the extra workload. You can see the latest employment laws on internships at **www.gov.uk/employment-rights-for-interns**.

www.internwise.co.uk

What is it?
The UK's number one intern recruitment site – you can find high-quality interns across every major skill sector.

What's free?
Posting an ad and accessing responses is free but the volume of responses is unlikely to be high unless you pay for your ad to be promoted.

> **top tip 1**
> It is free to register and post an ad but we recommend paying
> for your ad to be promoted by Internwise (£49.90 per ad), as
> it will generate a bigger and higher-quality pool of candidates
> to pick from.

> **top tip 2**
> If you get a lot of applications, do Skype interviews. They are a
> great way to select the candidates you want to interview face
> to face before you hire.

www.gumtree.com/jobs is also worth checking out, though
the quality of applicants does vary. Set a simple written task as a
screener – e.g. what is their point of view on your sector?

Odd jobs and freelancers

New digital services have made it easier than ever to find skilled
help for individual tasks or just a spare pair of hands for a small
odd job here or there:

www.fiverr.com

What is it?
A brilliant site to find a helping hand for odd jobs or small
business-related tasks.

What's free?
It is free to register but you will obviously have to pay the freelancers you hire.

> **top tip**
> Give a very clear written brief upfront that outlines the exact
> output you need.

www.peopleperhour.com

What is it?
A space to get freelancers for small jobs.

What's free?
Again it is free to register but you will need to pay the freelancers you use.

> **top tip**
> Request a proposal from a number of freelancers who have the relevant skill set and review for approach, capability and cost.

www.upwork.com

What is it?
Another freelancer recruitment website.

What's free?
It is free to register, but you then pay a 10 per cent fee on the value of the work you commission. There is a money-back guarantee if you aren't satisfied with the work you have commissioned.

> **top tip**
> While Upwork covers a wide range of sectors, it is a particularly good place to start if you are looking to find freelance developers (i.e. people who make websites) – it has the biggest pool of talent available.

Full-time employees

When the time comes for you to employ your first full-time employee then there are some excellent online services that will save you a fortune in recruitment fees. Here are three of the best:

www.linkedin.com/jobs

What is it?
The world's largest business social network with access to the

widest pool of talent. The place to begin your search for great candidates.

What's free?

It is free to set up and plan your job ad and LinkedIn offers good advice on how to write a compelling job post. But you will need to pay to make it go live.

top tip

Share your posted job with your LinkedIn connections, join relevant LinkedIn groups so your job is visible to its followers, add it to your profile status update and share the link to it on your other social media platforms.

Also look at **www.workinstartups.com**, which lets you post jobs and access a great pool of talent (with a more tech and digital focus).

https://angel.co is worth a look too. Primarily a site for pairing investors and start-ups, it also has a jobs section and is a great way to reach some of the best talent looking to work in start-ups.

Collaboration tools

Collaborating well will help you get maximum value from the people you work with, even if you live in different parts of the world. Here are some practical tools and services that will help you collaborate efficiently and effectively:

Project management

There are some excellent digital services that will help you manage projects and work streams. They are online systems which help you share information quickly, and stay in touch effortlessly. You always know who is doing what and you can collaborate on documents remotely.

Take your time to explore them and find the best solution for your needs.

www.dropbox.com

Sync, store and share files online for free. Dropbox seamlessly integrates onto your PC or Mac so you can access files instantly as well as automatically sync changes to important documents into the cloud.

www.google.com/docs

Another free file-sharing service, although we find this one less intuitive than Dropbox. You can invite your team to view, edit and comment on a document at any time. Useful for quickly finalizing shared documents.

https://trello.com

One of the best free project-managing tools. See everything that is happening with your project: What is most pressing? Who is working on what? What has already been completed?

www.muraly.com

An excellent free tool for creative collaboration, featuring a flexible shared canvas. Create shared mood boards, build ideas together, vote and prioritize. Fun and creative teamworking.

https://evernote.com

A brilliant free personal tool for capturing and organizing information and content of all kinds (text, video, audio, image, handwritten and web articles). Keep lists, collect inspiration and organize your thinking – and then share it.

www.wetransfer.com

A free (up to 10GB) large file-sharing service, that lets you password-protect and customize your files and messages. Links don't expire, which comes in handy when sharing files with large groups, some of whom may not need to access files immediately.

www.worksnaps.net

Track remote team workers' and freelancers' productivity on your project by accessing screen shots of their computer. A bit too Big Brother for some, but useful when you have a large disparate team.

www.rescuetime.com

A really smart tool for helping you increase your productivity by tracking your online behaviour and time spent on individual applications. It can be really useful to help individuals and small teams learn how to increase their productivity.

www.redmine.org

A free service for managing large teams of developers and detailed software builds. We wouldn't recommend it for managing normal projects as there are lots of simpler systems available, such as Trello.

https://basecamp.com

Basecamp is one of the best tools on the market for managing large projects such as events, software builds, marketing campaigns and product development. It offers a free sixty-day trial.

Staying in touch

Skype, FaceTime and Google Hangouts are still the best free solutions for simple day-to-day communication among remote team members. They have their limitations, though – in particular when it comes to large team interactions. Here are three free resources to fill those gaps:

www.freeconferencecall.com

What is it?
A reliable free conference-call service that works for domestic and international calls.

What's free?

The conference-call service is free, but to dial in participants have to call a toll number which is charged at their local network's rates.

> **top tip**
> They have a call-recording facility that can be really useful for interviews, legal calls or detailed client briefings.

www.gotomeeting.co.uk

What is it?

An HD online webinar, video-conferencing and meeting tool that is designed for hosting meetings of up to twenty-five people.

What's free?

It is a paid-for service – £29 a month – but they offer a full thirty-day free trial.

> **top tip**
> If you have a regular meeting you can set it up so that you can start it at the hit of a button – really useful if you want to check in quickly with your team.

www.hipchat.com

What is it?

A free instant-messaging service that lets your team communicate in real time.

What's free?

Everything!

> **top tip**
> You can also share, comment and collaborate on files, making HipChat a great instant-messaging tool for business.

Workspace

As your team grows, you might want to expand beyond the kitchen or café you have been working from, and find you have the money to invest in a larger space. When that happens, there are fully equipped and even quite fancy office spaces available for quite reasonable monthly rates.

Using flexible working spaces like the ones below is a good way to meet other creators and get access to professional office equipment without having to buy it. There are new ones springing up all the time, but here are some we have heard good things about:

www.impacthub.net

A global network of innovation and start-up communities (at time of writing there are sixty-three impact hubs open globally with five in the UK). Each of these offers working space as well as a range of other services from investment to incubation.

club.workspacegroup.co.uk

ClubWorkspace is a hot-desking and flexible working space for entrepreneurs and start-ups with ten fully kitted-out offices across London. Membership starts from £75 a month and increases depending on the location and amount of space you need.

www.rentadesk.co.uk

One location in central London and a range of pricing options – great if you need a space for an important meeting or interview.

estateoffice.com/containerville

Containerville is a new home for start-ups and small businesses by the Regents Canal in London. Thirty shipping containers arranged over two floors up-cycled into modern work spaces. Each container can accommodate up to eight desks.

7. FINDING INVESTMENT

You might choose or need to get investment in your idea. Investment from the right partners can be like rocket fuel for your business. It's worth noting, though, that things change the moment you do this. As soon as you borrow other people's money, you start to march to their tune as well as your own – so make sure this is something you want to do.

Putting the right investment strategy in place and managing potential and existing investors can be one of the more time-consuming tasks a creator experiences. It can detract focus from your idea, burn energy and, at worst, lock your idea into the wrong trajectory with the wrong partners. Before you do anything, do some learning. Speak to other creators who have raised money and get clear on what the long game looks like for you and your idea.

Here are a few good places to start learning:

fundersandfounders.com/how-funding-works-splitting-equity

A great source of information on funding and this blog post also has an awesome infographic on the rounds of funding available and how each works.

www.paulgraham.com/startupfunding.html

Written in 2005, Paul Graham's blog post on how start-up funding works is still one of the clearest and most useful explanations available.

www.f6s.com

A global community of founders, start-ups and angel investors. It is a useful shop window to meet potential angel investors but also to chat to founders in your sector who are raising capital now or have successfully raised it in the past.

The funding 'rounds'

There are essentially three standard rounds of funding that start-ups go through. Each has a different objective, a different 'ask' (i.e. how much is being borrowed) and a different portion of the equity of the business up for grabs.

Round 1 – Seed funding

What is it for? Small amounts of money that allow you and your team to work full-time on your idea to create a working proto-type and find the evidence that your idea has a fighting chance of succeeding. The latter might be a compelling set of user data, or crowds of people evidently paying for your service or product.

Who invests? Friends, family, crowdfunders (and sometimes angel investors).

The ask? This varies but seed funding is usually between £1,000 and £100,000 and is usually for a small chunk of equity in your idea (usually between 1 and 30 per cent), or sometimes it is just a simple loan.

Round 2 – Angel funding

What is it for? Your idea is not yet making enough money to take on bigger costs such as expanded product development, extra staff, sales and marketing budget. Funding will help you afford what you need to transform your idea from a promising proto-type into a revenue-generating and growing entity.

Who invests? Traditionally, this kind of investment comes from angel investors – wealthy individuals who may also have specialist knowledge and contacts in your field. Round 2 funding can also come from crowdfunding or VC (venture capital) companies, but for most creators this is pretty early to be getting into bed with a VC.

The ask? A sizeable chunk of money – often between £100,000 to £500,000 for between 10 and 40 per cent of your business.

Round 3 – Series A/B/C funding

What is it for? Now your business model is proven and your idea is making good money. You want to expand fast and go from money maker to market leader.

Who invests? Venture capitalists. These are companies that invest their own and other people's money in businesses they believe are set to grow. They will want to sell their stake in your business before long – either through an IPO (an initial public offering, where stock in your company is sold to institutional investors) or by selling to a competitor.

The ask? Usually in the millions, for a sizeable chunk of your business, often around a third, usually staged in a series of rounds.

What about crowdfunding?

Crowdfunding lets people invest directly in start-ups. Funding is raised from a large pool of people all investing small amounts. There are generally two types:

Reward based

Investors receive an incentive for investing a small sum but no equity. The two most popular platforms for this kind of crowdfunding are:

- **www.kickstarter.com** – receive funding by pre-selling your product, service or experience.
- **www.indiegogo.com** – raise funds through donations. This has a strong focus on the arts and creative projects.

Equity based

Investors receive equity in return for their investment. The two leading platforms for equity-based crowdfunding are:

- **www.crowdcube.com**, where, once your start-up is accepted onto their list, you can raise funds directly from professional investors and everyday folk looking to invest in start-ups.
- **www.seedrs.com**. A similar service to CrowdCube but with an emphasis on pre- and post-funding support for each of its funded start-ups.

top tip

Crowdfunding might seem like an easy way of raising money, but you will need to take a significant amount of time and care putting together a compelling pitch which convinces hundreds (sometimes thousands) of people to invest in your idea. You will also need to deliver on the promises you make, and communicate consistently with your many investors.

Angel investors

Angel investors are easily found with a quick Google search for 'business angels' or 'angel investors' in your sector.

There are also websites that match start-ups with angels. Four of the best for the UK are:

- **capitallist.com** – A great shop window to quickly get your idea in front of lots of London-based angels. They also offer fundraising consulting services as well as meet-ups with other entrepreneurs as well as investors.
- **https://angel.co** and **www.angelsden.com** – Both very similar to Capital List but with a global reach.
- **www.angelcofund.co.uk** – A syndicate of private investors looking to invest in small and medium-sized businesses.

For sound advice on how to find business angels, syndicates and networks, try **www.ukbusinessangelsassociation.org.uk**. Even better, go to one of their 'Introduction to Angel Investing' events.

It's worth knowing that some angel networks charge a fee for you to pitch your idea – this is intended to focus you on giving a presentation investors want to see, so make sure you want investment from that particular network before you pitch.

Writing investment proposals

Investors generally expect an investment proposal. This is a document making the case for why your idea is worth investing in. It should contain inspiring information: on you, your idea, the problem it is solving and why it is better than the competition, and the commercial case for investment.

Investors want to be able to understand how your idea makes money, why you need investment and how much you need, and when they can expect to get their money back.

A sensible investor will be just as interested in you, assuming it will be you who leads the business to the point where they increase the value of their investment. Tell them about your passion for the idea, the journey you have been on and your intentions for the future.

The best way to learn about how to write a great proposal is to chat to other creators who have already raised money. You can also find an expert on preparing investor proposals at a freelance site like **www.upwork.com** – someone who will help you edit and structure your proposal.

Here are three more online resources about how to do this phase of your idea's growth well:

- **www.venturegiant.com/news-channel-365-how-to-write-the-perfect-investment-proposal---investment-proposal-template.aspx**
- **www.entrepreneurmag.co.za/advice/funding/attracting-investors/how-to-write-a-funding-proposal/**
- **www.sequoiacap.com/grove/posts/6bzx/writing-a-business-plan**

8. BORING BUT IMPORTANT

There are parts of making an idea happen that aren't glamorous, fun or particularly fulfilling, but you have to do them. Below are some of the best resources, many of them free, that we have found for taking care of these business essentials professionally and with minimum fuss.

Legal advice and contracts

www.docracy.com

What is it?
Free legal documents that are useful for start-ups, curated and regularly updated by the Docracy community. Documents range from employee contracts through to founder equity share agreements.

What's free?
The service is completely free – to access, store and edit legal documents.

> **top tip**
> The one thing that Docracy can't help you with is knowing with certainty that the legal document you are using is the right one. If in doubt, get a second opinion from a qualified lawyer who specializes in the relevant field.

www.echosign.adobe.com

What is it?
An app that lets you attach e-signature functionality to your online contracts so that they can be signed instantly by the receiver.

What's free?

It is a paid-for service (prices vary based on volume – the basic package is $14 a month) but they offer a free fourteen-day trial.

top tip
Adobe Echosign integrates into Salesforce so can be a useful way to shorten your sales cycle and make tracking and managing contracts and invoicing simpler.

www.companiesmadesimple.com

What is it?

A great resource for incorporating a UK company – do it all online for £16.99.

What's free?

It costs from £16.99 to create a limited company using Companies Made Simple (including the Companies House filing fee). They also offer a free start-up toolkit including useful info to help you run your new business effectively.

top tip
Before you incorporate your company, check with an accountant that it's the right thing to do. From a taxation point of view, there are advantages as well as disadvantages related to remaining a sole trader or partnership.

Bookkeeping

www.xero.com

What is it?

Cloud-based accounting software for small to medium-sized businesses specializing in invoicing, bank reconciliation and bookkeeping.

What's free?
The starter package is $20 a month – for small volumes of invoices, bills and bank payments. They offer a free thirty-day trial.

www.kashflow.com

What is it?
A cloud-based accounting and bookkeeping platform for start-ups – a comparable service to Xero but the entry-level package is cheaper.

What's free?
The basic package is £5 a month and they offer a free fourteen-day trial.

> **top tip**
> Check out the purchase automation feature – useful if you need to make recurring purchases from suppliers.

Billing and invoicing

www.slimvoice.co

What is it?
SlimVoice is a simple way of doing online invoices. It sends an invoice direct to the client without you needing to generate a PDF.

What's free?
It is a free service.

> **top tip**
> Since you own your invoicing data and history, you can download and access it whenever you need – like when you're doing your tax return.

invoiceto.me and **https://invoice-generator.com** are two other free online invoice-generating services that are worth a try.

www.getballpark.com

What is it?
Ballpark is a time-tracking and invoicing service that is great if you are self-employed and bill other people for your time.

What's free?
A login for one user costs $12.99 a month and you get access to all functionality for that. They also offer a free thirty-day trial.

> **top tip**
> Do time-tracking and invoicing in one. This makes bookkeeping and tax returns easier to process – perfect if your idea involves you selling your (or other people's) time.

www.chargebee.com

What is it?
An online billing platform for subscription businesses to let you set up, track and manage regular billing of customers.

What's free?
The start-up package starts at $49 a month and lets you charge up to fifty invoices a month. They also offer a free trial.

> **top tip**
> You can run trials and do configurable pricing, which is very handy for more sophisticated subscription business models.

Good Luck!

We hope that you find this list useful as you build your idea. Please let us know if any of it needs updating, or you find something we are recommending doesn't work as you'd hoped. Also, if you discover other resources which we should tell creators about, please let us know about them. We want The Creator's Black Book to be the most valuable list of resources around.

Good luck on this incredible journey of making your idea happen!

acknowledgements

We would like to thank these people for helping us:

Annie Hollands
Ben Chappell
Bethan John
Bunmi Western
Charlie Dark
Ed Foy
Ed Pellew
Ed Smith
Emma Brown
Emma-Jayne Parkes
Faisel Rahman
Fi Star-Stone
Georgie Reames
Giles English
Harriot Pleydell-Bouverie
Hatty Kingsley-Miller
James Ashworth
James Elliot
James Kennedy
James Wills
Jane ní Dhulchaointigh

Joel Rickett
Kathryn Parsons
Mark Johnson
Matt Judkins
Mo Saha
Nick Peperell
Paul Sinton-Hewitt
Richard Lennon
Richard Mills
Richard Reed
Richard Wilkinson
Sean Collins
Shaz Saleem
Thom Elliot
Tom Mercer
Trevor Horwood
Vishal Amin
Zach Klein
Zoe Bohm